POLITICS IN MINUTES

MARCUS WEEKS

POLITICS IN MINUTES

MARCUS WEEKS

Quercus

CONTENTS

Introduction

A surprisingly large proportion of people profess to have no interest in politics. Yet in conversations in bars and cafés, over dinner tables, and at the water cooler, it's difficult to find someone who doesn't have an opinion on the news of the day. The substance of these informal discussions and arguments is the same as the debates that are held in parliaments and in the media: the best way to organize the society we live in. In short, politics.

Politics affects every aspect of our lives, and whether we know it or not. We all take an interest in the ways society impinges on our freedoms, protects us from harm, or allows us to get on with our lives. Simply by living in a society, we are taking part in a political process – choosing how that society should be organized, governed, and regulated is the business of politics. The rules and regulations, rights and responsibilities, and duties and benefits, are the nuts and bolts of politics; how they are decided and by whom the stuff of political philosophy.

Few subjects – except perhaps sport or religion – arouse such passion as politics. Followers of any particular political party or ideology can show as much loyalty as others do to their local football team, and have absolute faith in its validity. Differences of opinion range from the polite disagreement of the dinner-party discussion, to a clash of cultures and all-out war.

Arguments by politicians and their supporters from all sides of the political spectrum are aimed to persuade us to their point of view, and news stories in the media are all presented from a necessarily biased perspective. Rather than simply accepting the political opinions being touted by those seeking our vote or pushing a political agenda, most of us like to think we can make up our own minds. But in order to do that, we need to be aware of all the options, the thinking behind them and their implications. The ideas briefly presented in this little book will go some way to help the reader formulate rational political views, or at least have an informed justification for the beliefs he or she already holds and, hopefully, to approach the ballot box with more conviction and confidence. And, of course, to be more persuasive in the debates at the bar or water cooler.

The evolution of politics

'Man', the philosopher Aristotle asserted, 'is a political animal.' What he meant is that humans are by nature social, and tend to live and work together in groups, and in order to function properly, these groups need to have an underlying political system. Family groups have, over time, developed into tribal communities, villages, towns and eventually cities and states. In order for the members of these societies to function as a unit, there had to be some organization, and an authority to ensure the well-being of the group.

In primitive family groups – as with pack animals – the ruler was often the patriarch, the alpha male. As these groups became larger and more sophisticated, so too did the systems used to organize and regulate them; in addition to the single leader there developed ruling families and councils of elders. Some rulers inherited their position; others were appointed for their leadership qualities. Even before the founding of the first great civilizations, the elements of politics had begun to evolve.

Government and leadership

Civilization came with the establishment of settled communities – towns and cities, and eventually nation states and empires. For these societies to thrive, they needed a more formal system of organization than the absolute rule of a tribal leader. This required formulating rules and regulations, and the means to enforce them – the business of government. Among other things, governments have the authority to make and enforce laws, collect taxes and order military forces. Who acquires and administers this power is the business of politics.

Modern societies are more often than not governed by a group of people. The notion of leadership runs deep in the human psyche, however, and there are still some states in the world ruled by a single leader, whether a benign monarch or tyrannical dictator. Even democracies with governments of elected representatives feel the need for a symbolic figurehead, and there is almost invariably a head of state in the form of a monarch, president or prime minister.

Hierarchies

The larger and more sophisticated a society becomes, the more complex its organizational structures tend to be. Small tribal groups consisted simply of a single leader and his people – the ruler and the ruled – but modern nation states and even local communities have outgrown this simple model. Hierarchies of various sorts have evolved, with different levels of power and authority. A medieval monarch, for example, sat at the top of the pecking order, but between him and the ordinary serfs were the noble families of the aristocracy, given some power by the king in return for certain favours.

The pattern of hierarchies continues today in the pyramid-like structures of governments, with citizens forming the base, and layers of government such as civil servants, parliament and ministers above them, and at the apex the head of state. The effectiveness of such a political hierarchy is determined by how much power is imposed by any level on those below, and how much authority is given by the lower levels to those above.

Kings/
Monarchs

Barons/Nobles

Knights

Peasants

The Greeks and
the city-state

It is something of a truism to say that political thought had its origins in Ancient Greece, and that classical Athenians 'invented democracy'. But it would be more accurate to say that in the 6th century BCE, Athens had become the centre of a prosperous city-state, with an educated urban population. Philosophical debate flourished, including discussions of how the state should be governed, and in 510 BCE the ruling tyrant was deposed and political power was given to the people. Or, at least, some of the people.

Decisions about the running of the state were made by popular assembly, which all eligible male citizens were encouraged to attend. The fledgling democracy, the first of its kind, inspired ordinary citizens to consider what sort of society they would like to live in, and how it should be administered. At the same time, Athens fostered an atmosphere of intellectual enquiry, producing philosophers including Socrates, Plato and Aristotle – from which evolved the beginnings of political philosophy.

Plato: *Republic*

One of the first questions for the early Greek political philosophers was: what is the purpose of government? Until then, it had been taken for granted that a community should have a leader but, now power had been transferred to the people, Athenian thinkers began to ask what sort of society and what kind of government would be best. Plato, in his book *Republic*, argued that the role of government is to ensure that citizens are able to pursue a 'good life' – not simply one of pleasure or happiness, but also a virtuous one.

The only people with the insight needed to recognize and understand the virtues that constitute a good life, and the wisdom to put them into practice, however, are philosophers. Ordinary people have only a shadowy knowledge of these concepts and require guidance to lead a good life. This, Plato said, is the role of government, and the only people qualified to provide it are philosophers: government should therefore be in the hands of a guardian class of 'philosopher-kings'.

Aristotle: *Politics*

Plato's pupil Aristotle was altogether more methodical than his mentor in his approach to the question of government. First of all, he tried to determine all possible forms of government and then assess the merits of each to determine the optimum form. Aristotle used two criteria: who rules? and for whose benefit? In answer to the second question, he identified two possible answers. Either the government was in the interest of the state as a whole (what he called true government), or in the interest of those in power (corrupt government). As for the first question, he thought government could be by an individual ruler, a small ruling elite or the people. Aristotle settled on three possible forms of 'true government' (royalty, aristocracy or constitutional polity) and three 'corrupt governments' (tyranny, oligarchy and democracy). Of these, he considered government by the people for the common good as the most desirable, but distinguished this from his second-best choice – democracy – government by the people in their own individual interest.

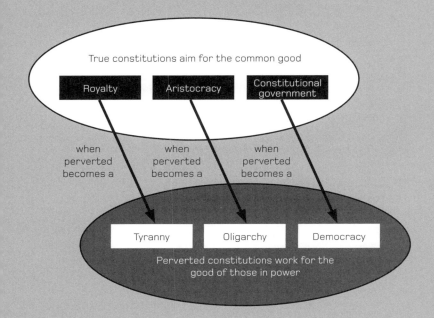

Civil society

Politics, contrary to the impression most people have, is not confined to the activities of political parties and the business of government. While government makes and administers the laws affecting society as a whole, there are also organizations, associations, communities and networks – separate from commercial business and the state – that form around a common interest or activity.

These social groups operate in the sphere between the individual and the state known as civil society. They include religious and charitable organizations, sporting and social associations, and local community groups, but also movements with more specific objectives. These are often referred to as NGOs (non-governmental organizations), and many of them campaign to influence government policy on specific issues, such as the environment, health or human rights. Some, such as Greenpeace and Oxfam, have become large international organizations, while others exert only local influence.

Human nature

The democracies of classical Greece and Rome were comparatively short-lived, and when their republics reverted to monarchies, philosophical discussion of different forms of government all but disappeared. The legitimacy of royal rule was eventually challenged, and with the Enlightenment came a new interest in political philosophy. The English philosopher Thomas Hobbes set the agenda by asking the fundamental question of why we need government at all. How, he asked, would we humans live in a 'state of nature'? Having lived through the brutal English Civil War, he had a cynical view of human nature, and believed that left to their own devices humans would be in a state of continual conflict, and life would be 'solitary, poor, nasty, brutish, and short.' Government is necessary to prevent us reverting to this state of nature, and according to Hobbes should be in the form of an authoritarian ruler. Other political philosophers, such as John Locke and Jean-Jacques Rousseau, had a less jaundiced view of human nature, and the forms of government best suited to it.

Representation

Direct democracy, such as the government of classical Athens, is based on the idea that the people can all play an active part in the political process, each having an equal say in determining the rules governing their society. But while it is possible to call regular meetings of all citizens to decide matters in small communities, it is not a practicable system for governing a city, let alone a nation.

To overcome this problem, groups of citizens were given the right to elect someone to represent their views and act on their behalf, in meetings with representatives of other groups. From these meetings of representatives developed a more complex system of representative democracy, in which local areas elect representatives to regional assemblies and to national parliaments. The idea of direct democracy has not been completely superseded, however. On some issues of particular importance, the public is consulted as a whole and all eligible voters are asked for their opinion in a referendum.

Authority and legitimacy; power and accountability

The majority of political thinkers (with the notable exception of anarchists, see page 228) have acknowledged the necessity of some form of government. But a government can only rule effectively if its power is recognized and respected by the citizens. A government must have authority, but this alone does not make it a legitimate government – tyrannical dictators, for example, impose rule by force. In contrast, an elected government given a mandate by the electorate has effectively been granted the power to rule.

What's more, if there are regular elections, or some other means of removing a government or its members from office, there is a system of accountability. The great majority of political systems worldwide are based on these principles of authority, legitimacy and accountability. The differences between them are a matter of degree – the amount of power granted by the people to their government, how much their authority is open to abuse, and how easily they can be removed.

Sovereignty

The legitimate authority to rule within a territory that a government or ruler has is sometimes referred to as sovereignty: the right to govern. In the ancient world, an emperor was acknowledged as the absolute ruler, or sovereign power, and this concept was later transferred to the authority granted by a people to its government. But the notion of sovereignty has wider implications in international affairs. An agreement reached by European leaders in the Peace of Westphalia in 1648 established an important principle of sovereign government: that it should be allowed to have authority over its own territory and people without interference from outside. A sovereign government should be free to make and enforce laws within its own territories, and no outsider should attempt to disrupt a sovereign government, nor attempt to enter or cross any of its sovereign territory without permission. Opinions of what constitutes legitimate authority differ widely, however, as do justifications for interference in the internal affairs of other states.

The role of religion

In early societies, rulers were often both spiritual and political leaders, and the connection has persisted in some to this day. Medieval Europe was effectively ruled by the Christian church, led by a Pope and monarchs with a 'divine right' to rule; the Prophet Muhammad established an Islamic Empire as well as the religion of Islam. Religious differences have also shaped national borders – as when Orthodox and Catholic churches divided, in the partition of India, and the creation of the state of Israel — and have been the ostensible grounds for conflict. From the Renaissance period onwards, humanist ideas came to the fore, the old monarchies lost power to more democratic governments, and religion was seen as something separate from politics. Many new republics established in the 18th and 19th centuries were avowedly secular states (while advocating religious tolerance) and in some communist states of the 20th century religion was outlawed. Nevertheless, religious belief is a potent force – some nations have an official state religion; others, such as the UK, have an established Church.

Political ideologies: left and right

The Age of Enlightenment brought with it a renewed interest in political philosophy, as increasingly nations rejected monarchical models and sought to establish new forms of government. Inevitably, there was a wide range of opinions of how this was to be best achieved, and a number of distinct political ideologies developed. Some thinkers advocated radical changes, while others advised retaining tried and tested models. During the French Revolution, members of the parliament who supported the monarchy of the Ancien Régime sat to the right of the president, and those who sought a democratic republic on the left. This arrangement gave rise to the terms right-wing and left-wing to describe the conservative and progressive political movements respectively. Broadly speaking, the right wing favours policies based on protection of the freedoms of the individual, private ownership and minimal taxes and intervention. In contrast, the left wing is generally in favour of collectivity, equality, public ownership and the provision of social welfare through taxation.

Political ideologies: the political spectrum

The classification of political ideologies as either left- or right-wing, or at least as being at some point on a scale that ranges from communism at one end and fascism at the other, is, of course, an oversimplification. The criteria for determining a place on the political spectrum are both economic and social, and a political movement may be socially conservative and economically progressive, or vice versa.

Another factor that should perhaps be taken into account is the degree to which a political party dictates and interferes in the activities of the people – how authoritarian or libertarian it is. In the modern world, liberal democracies of one kind or another are the norm, with some form of social welfare, as well as a more or less laissez-faire attitude to free-market capitalism, and the predominant political ideologies are clustered around the centre of the left–right scale. The differences between them can be more clearly seen if each aspect of their policies is examined separately.

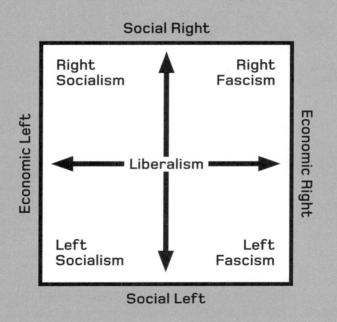

Political concepts

Much of the study of politics concerns the 'nuts and bolts' of government, examining the way that states and communities are organized and governed in practice. But there is also a theoretical side to politics attempting to answer basic questions about the fundamental concepts underlying political thought. Political theory has its roots in the political philosophy of the ancient world. Classical Greek philosophers in particular examined notions such as justice, equality, freedom and authority. An understanding of these was recognized as crucial to the business of politics, and for determining the purpose of government and providing a rationale for possible structures of governance. Definitions of these fundamental concepts, however, have proved elusive. The various interpretations have given rise to a wide range of political opinions and systems of government. The field of political theory emerged to propose practical applications for this political philosophy offering different models of society and how it should be governed, as well as the things that government should concern itself with.

Ancient Greek ideas of justice and liberty

At the heart of Ancient Greek political thought was the concept of *eudaemonia*, the 'good life'. People live together in societies for their mutual benefit, in order to live good and happy lives; these societies need to be organized and have rules and therefore it is the purpose of the state and its government to ensure it. Whatever the constitution of the government, it should protect its citizens from harm and prevent injustice and infringements of their freedom.

Philosophers, such as Socrates and Plato, argued that justice was a virtue, and as such was closely linked to the notion of what is good. On a personal level, a citizen is just if he acts virtuously and does what is good, so for a government to be just it too must act with an understanding of what is good. However, the concept of 'virtue', and therefore justice, is open to interpretation, and even a just government was somewhat at odds with the Greek idea of liberty – the freedom to lead one's life as one likes, independent of any master.

Site of the Areopagus,
the high court of Athens .

Feudalism

Although a number of more or less democratic republics were established in the ancient world, they were the exception rather than the rule. Even the Roman Republic, modelled on the Greek republics it succeeded, eventually handed power to a single dictator – Julius Caesar, the first of a line of Roman emperors. Christianity was slowly adopted as the official religion of the Roman Empire, spreading the influence of the Roman church, both spiritual and political. In medieval Europe, the Church, with the Pope at its head, exerted considerable political power.

The predominant social order was a hierarchical system of property ownership and duty known as feudalism. At the head of the state was an absolute monarch, owner and ruler of all the land. The monarch granted some of the land to a class of nobles, who in return provided him with fighting forces; the nobles granted some of their land to vassals in return for an oath of loyalty, and it was ultimately worked by a class of serfs.

Humanism and the rise of the nation state

The Renaissance marked the beginning of the end for the feudal systems of the Middle Ages. An increasingly prosperous urban population in Europe was founded on trade rather than agriculture, and with it came an intellectual revolution which threw doubt on the old certainties of religion and tradition. Scientific discoveries and the rediscovery of classical philosophical ideas contradicted religious dogma, and challenged the power of the Church and monarchs.

Humanism put Man rather than God at the centre of political thinking. Starting in 15th-century Italy, a number of republics were established, with laws and government devised by the people rather than divinely dictated. Elsewhere in Europe, other countries began to assert their independence from the Holy Roman Empire as sovereign nation states, although few opted to become republics and retained their monarchies. The traditional hierarchies of aristocracy lingered until a spirit of republicanism resurfaced during the Enlightenment.

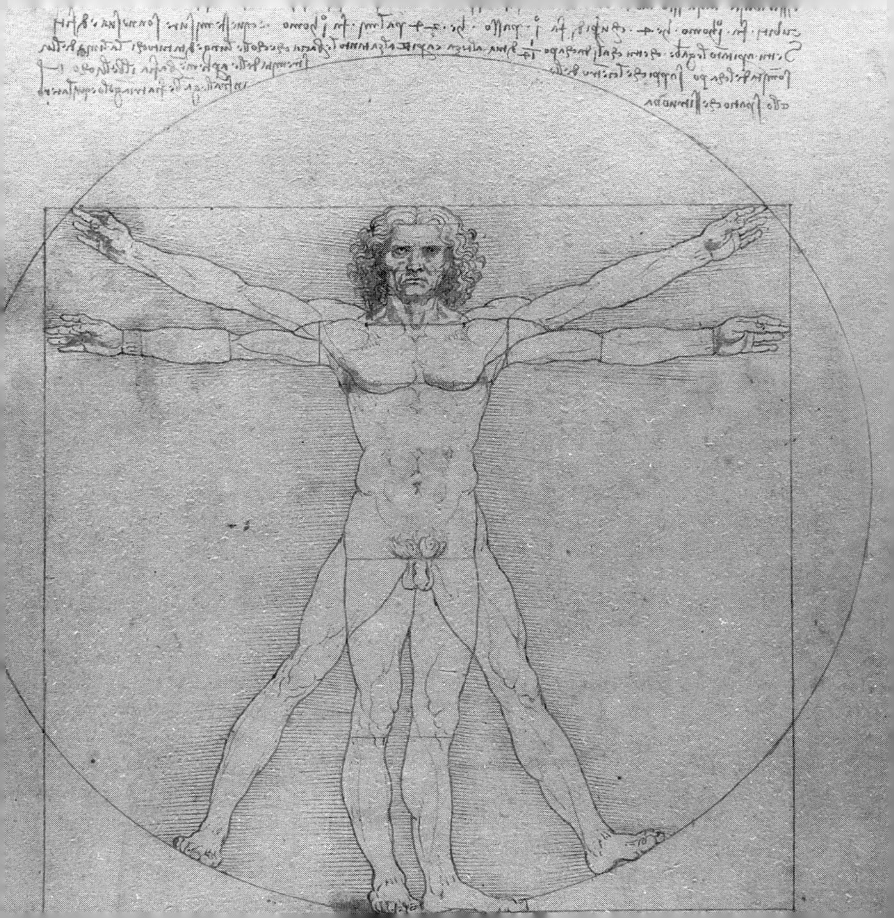

Machiavelli and political realism

The humanism associated with Renaissance political philosophy instilled the idea that it is people, not God, that determine our politics, decide our laws and how we should be governed. Humans, however, have flaws and live in an imperfect world. Accordingly, the Renaissance humanist Niccolò Machiavelli (pictured) suggested that rather than philosophizing about an ideal form of government in an ideal state, we should be realistic – see things as they are, rather than how they should be. He argued in *The Prince* that morality and ethics are all very well for individuals, but in government the wellbeing of the state is paramount and should be pursued by any means necessary – ethical or unethical. In short, the ends justify the means. Subterfuge, lying and even violence are legitimate tactics for a ruler or government if the outcome is favourable to the state. Machiavelli stripped political philosophy of its ethics and ideology, influencing a movement of political realism, which was adopted by Thomas Hobbes and later resurfaced in the *Realpolitik* of 19th-century Germany.

Enlightenment

The so-called Age of Reason, or Enlightenment, that spanned the 17th and 18th centuries was an extraordinary period of intellectual and cultural activity in Europe. Scientists and philosophers in France and Britain introduced new ideas based on rational thought rather than faith. With this resurgence of philosophical enquiry came a renewed interest in political philosophy and a re-evaluation of the traditional forms of government. The Enlightenment notion of reason as a basis for reform led to an emphasis on the ideals of liberty and justice, and increasing demands for democracy and citizens' rights.

In France, in particular, thinkers such as Voltaire (pictured) and Jean-Jacques Rousseau advocated a complete change to the old, discredited systems of government, inspiring a movement that culminated in the French Revolution and the formation of the République, and American Independence. Enlightenment ideals sowed the seeds of revolution, but also laid the foundations of modern political philosophy.

Concept of liberty

Jean-Jacques Rousseau's famous statement that 'Man was born free, but everywhere he is in chains' was the rallying cry of revolutionary movements in the 18th and 19th centuries. Yet it harked back to the concepts of liberty and slavery that underpinned classical ideas of democracy – rule imposed on citizens is a restriction of freedom and the mark of the slave. Rousseau believed that laws and systems of government had evolved primarily to protect property, and restricted the natural freedom of people. But exactly what are the freedoms that we want to enjoy, and how can they be protected?

Without some restrictions, it is impossible to maintain order, as freedoms can be open to abuse. One person's liberty may impinge on another's freedoms. And there are different aspects of liberty, such as economic and social freedoms. Replacing the old order of monarchies offered the opportunity to rethink ideas of liberty, and a number of libertarian options emerged as an alternative to conservative authoritarianism.

Positive and negative freedom

The concept of liberty was extensively examined by 19th-century political philosophers, notably John Stuart Mill (see page 158), and its various interpretations became the basis for liberalism, laissez-faire capitalism and anarchism. If there was disagreement about how liberty was granted in practice, it was generally accepted that it entailed freedom from constraint. In the 1950s, the liberal philosopher Isaiah Berlin gave a lecture titled *Two Concepts of Liberty*. The traditional view of liberty, he argued, is negative liberty – freedom from outside interference. It is the aim of liberal political ideologies to minimize the restrictions preventing people from doing things. There is, however, another sort of liberty – positive liberty. This is the freedom an individual has to do something, rather than simply not being prevented from doing it. Berlin believed that government should protect negative liberty and foster positive liberty, encouraging people to be in control of their own lives and fulfil their potential. This is not without risk as Berlin pointed out: 'Freedom for the pike is death for the minnows.'

Concept of justice

Just as the concept of liberty was re-examined in the late 20th century, so too was there a reappraisal of the notion of justice. In the US in the 1970s, Johns Rawls and Robert Nozick presented interpretations that encapsulated respectively contemporary liberal-left and conservative-right thinking on the issue of the just distribution of wealth. In *A Theory of Justice*, Rawls uses a thought experiment in which we are invited to construct a society from scratch, but from behind a 'veil of ignorance' as to how privileged each one of us is at the start. To avoid the risk of being part of a poor underclass, he argues, we opt for a fair and reasonably equal distribution. The essence of social justice, he concludes, is fairness. In reply to this, Nozick presented his argument that a distribution of goods is just when it arises from exchanges freely entered into. This may end up in inequalities, with some doing better from the deals than others, but unless it is a result of theft, fraud or coercion, the distribution is just. Justice, says Rawls, is a matter of entitlement, not fairness.

Equality: of outcome or opportunity?

The notion of equality is closely linked to ideas of justice and fairness. Equality was the watchword of the revolutionary movements in France and America, expressed explicitly in the US Declaration of Independence in the statement, 'We hold these truths to be self-evident, that all men are created equal'. Since then, it has become a cornerstone of human rights. However, it is easier to recognize than to define.

While it is generally agreed that all citizens should be equally subject to the law, and even that there should be equality of opportunity, there are differences of opinion about wealth distribution. A wholly egalitarian society arguably removes the incentive for improvement. Also, those whose achievements contribute most to society should be rewarded most. But deciding who is deserving and who undeserving, is a contentious matter. Growing inequality, both within societies and between rich and poor nations, is forcing political thinkers to re-examine the practicalities of a more egalitarian society.

The social contract

With the formation of new nation states came the opportunity to decide their form of government. It also prompted thinkers to examine the more fundamental questions of why government is necessary, and the relationship between its power and the rights of the citizens. At the heart of this was the realization that social order and law, like society itself, are human creations, and depend on a consensus. Enlightenment political philosophers, including Hugo Grotius, Thomas Hobbes, John Locke and Jean-Jacques Rousseau, believed that a legitimate government is granted its power by a 'social contract': the citizens agree to surrender some of their liberty and submit to the authority of the government in return for protection of their other rights. Hobbes saw this as a way of maintaining social order, with the people abdicating their rights to an absolute sovereign, while Rousseau emphasized the idea of consensus, where individual citizens submitted to the 'general will'. Locke's position came somewhere in between, arguing that a government protects the 'natural rights' of its citizens and arbitrates civil disputes.

Political authority

The 'social contract' between the governed and the government concerns, on the one hand, the rights of the individual and, on the other, the power of the state. With the consensus of the individuals, a ruler or government is given the authority to govern, make laws, levy taxes and so on. This is often formalized explicitly in a constitution, which details the extent of the government's authority and its obligations.

A government can rely on a number of autonomous agencies – police and armed forces, and revenue collection and border agencies – to enforce its will. However, the legitimacy of a government's authority is dependent on it not abusing these powers, as well as fulfilling its side of the agreement. Despotic leaders or corrupt governments will be reluctant to relinquish power, and abuse the authority given by the people to hold on to it. Regular elections, which can be seen as renewals of the agreement, allow a degree of accountability, as can the separation of powers (see page 128).

Rights: civil and natural

The concept of rights, especially as a factor in the social contract, was central to Enlightenment political philosophy. Several thinkers suggested that there are certain basic expectations of life to which every individual is entitled. Hobbes argued that in a 'state of nature', it is every man for himself so these rights could only exist with a strong government. Locke's view, however – later echoed in the US Declaration of Independence – was that there are certain natural, inalienable rights which could not be surrendered to governments, including the rights to life, liberty and the pursuit of happiness. But as well as these natural rights, which some saw as God-given, there are other rights granted by man-made laws. These civil rights include the right to own property, to participate in the political process by voting and to have access to a court of law. Both natural rights and civil rights may be specified in the formal constitution of a state, or in a separate bill of rights, and are together considered as human rights recognized by individual states and international conventions.

Frontispiece of *Leviathan*, Thomas Hobbes's influential book pubished in 1651 following the English Civil War.

Influencing politics

Societies that have some form of elected government implicitly acknowledge the need for governance, and more often than not specify in law how it should be constituted and the limits of its power. Opinions among the people will differ, however, and this is reflected in the ideology of the governments they elect. Naturally, political parties and their activists will try to influence public opinion especially at election time.

At the same time, there are groups with particular interests, who campaign to influence government policy. These advocacy groups can exert some influence through lobbying, but more controversially also through donations to political parties, or sponsoring candidates to elections. Although special interest groups can highlight matters of public concern – moral, religious or environmental issues, for example – political and commercial special interest groups can influence the political process, with the risk of unfair manipulation and even corruption.

Freedom of speech

A defining aspect of liberty is the freedom to hold an opinion and express it openly. Freedom of speech – and especially freedom to publish – has been considered the mark of a civilized society since the Enlightenment, when dissenting voices challenged the authority of the old order. This freedom highlights a fundamental problem of liberty in general: if it is permissible to say anything, then some people will say things that others will find unacceptable, summed up in Voltaire's famous dictum 'I disapprove of what you say, but I will defend to the death your right to say it' (actually written by his biographer Evelyn Beatrice Hall). Oppressive regimes quash opposition by restricting the freedoms of the press, but even in societies that pride themselves on their liberal principles, there is often some form of censorship. This may be benign in intent, protecting minors or preventing incitement to violence, for example. More contentious are laws such as those banning Holocaust denial, or blasphemy. These ideas may cause offence, but is that sufficient reason to outlaw them?

The right to protest

In most modern liberal democracies, political parties contest elections to form the government. In this way, as well as a ruling party (or coalition of parties) there are elected representatives in opposition, to argue for those who hold different views. But individuals also feel the need to oppose governments, and in many societies there is a right to free speech and the right to protest. The degree to which it allows criticism and protest is often the test of a civilized society.

Authoritarian states may restrict citizens' rights to voice criticism of the establishment or hold demonstrations, but in others the right to protest is specifically enshrined in law. But even in liberal countries, these rights can be limited by law. Of course, violent and destructive protest is outlawed, but restrictions on public gatherings have been introduced in some places, justified by concerns of law and order. Recently, concerns of terrorism have led to certain organizations also being outlawed and restrictions imposed on communications.

Peaceful protest and civil disobedience

While large organizations and powerful individuals can influence governments and make their views known in the media, other interest groups – especially those with less financial resources – may highlight their concerns through some form of direct action. Frequently, this takes the form of public gatherings, a protest march, such as Gandhi's famous 1930 Salt March in India, a sit-in, or presenting a petition. These demonstrations are generally peaceful and legal, although there may be public order restrictions on the number of people involved and the amount of disruption they cause.

Other forms of direct action specifically break a law considered unjust. This civil disobedience ranges from non-cooperation, such as withdrawal of labour, through conscientious objection by non-payment of taxes, refusal to serve on juries or in the armed forces, to symbolic acts of minor vandalism, which may include computer hacking. Whistle-blowing exposes corruption and abuse of power with evidence from an inside source.

Violent direct action

Frustration with the actions of a government can often trigger a shift from peaceful protest and civil disobedience to more violent direct action, particularly when that government is oppressive or corrupt. It is also common for peaceful demonstrations to become violent when feelings run high or their policing is heavy-handed. Although usually seen as a last resort, actions such as rioting, destruction of property and even terrorism and assassination are seen by extremist movements as legitimate forms of protest.

These may be isolated instances of terrorism, such as bombings or hostage-taking, or part of a campaign of armed insurrection involving military action against government forces. Depending on the circumstances, and the political leanings of the observer, the use of violence can be seen as a cowardly attack on democratic values or the heroic actions of freedom fighters – yet mainstream political ideologies are reluctant to condone the use of force except as a last resort.

Revolution

When the government of a democratic state loses popular support, it can be removed in an election. But if a government holds on to power when a significant proportion of citizens are impatient for change, the protest may escalate and force the overthrow of the regime, more often than not with a radical shift in the social order. Such socio-political revolutions have occurred throughout history, but became more prevalent in the 18th and 19th centuries when monarchies were toppled and colonial rulers ousted in the establishment of democratic republics, such as France and the USA.

In some cases the movement for change is great enough for revolution to be swift and bloodless, in others the state is so divided that there is a civil war, or a substantial faction at war. The term 'revolution' is generally used to refer to a popular revolt against a despotic ruler or government, in contrast to the 'top-down' seizure of power from a democratic government, a coup d'état, by a dictator or military force (see page 262).

Structures and institutions

Although political philosophers focus on the theory of government or ideology, there is also the very practical business of how any form of government operates in practice – the systems, structures and institutions through which it conducts its business. The processes, institutions and behaviour of a government are sometimes known as 'governance' to distinguish it from the governing body itself.

The most obvious institutions are housed in the seats of government, often in imposing buildings, such as royal palaces or parliament buildings. But other government departments occupy offices, town halls and courts of law. These visible signs of systems and structures allow a government to run a state by administering its economic, social and foreign policies, and enforcing its laws. And while the extent of these bureaucratic systems differs from state to state, the basic structures and institutions are similar no matter what form of government, and no matter what political ideology it represents.

Government by the few

Some institutions of government evolve from practical necessity, rather than from political theory. This is also true of government itself. For most of history, 'government' meant the rule of a single monarch or ruling aristocracy – not much different from a patriarchal tribal leader. 'Monarchy' literally means 'rule by one individual' but has developed into the idea of a ruling king or queen. Similarly, 'tyrant' and 'dictator' were originally neutral descriptions of single leaders, but have taken on a negative, pejorative meaning. The modern connotation of these terms reflects a changing perception of the desirability of an absolute ruler, and only a handful of absolute monarchies exist today in Brunei, Qatar, Oman, Saudi Arabia, Swaziland, the UAE and Vatican City. However, even democracies show a need for a single figurehead. Several countries retain a royal family in a system of constitutional monarchy, where the monarch's role is largely ceremonial and symbolic. And even in republics, the idea of a single leader lingers in the election of a president or head of state.

Government by the people

While the idea of monarchy or a single leader evolved from ancient traditions, the advent of political philosophy challenged the status quo. Thinkers began to examine other alternatives to hereditary patriarchy. Might it be better, for instance, to appoint leaders on merit, not by accident of birth?

From this developed the idea of making conscious decisions about the form of government a society should have and the participation of the people in making that choice. In Ancient Greece and then in Rome, the old tyrants were deposed and replaced with republics, and medieval Europe saw a very gradual decline in the power of the monarchies in favour of greater democracy. Some form of democracy, with the people participating to some degree in the way in which they are governed, today forms part of almost all modern mainstream political ideologies, and so is arguably as much an institution as an ideology – or at least is the raison d'être of institutions, such as parliaments and congresses.

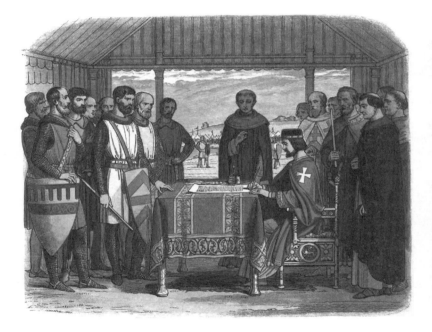

Bureaucracy

The word 'bureaucracy' has unfortunately earned a negative connotation, that of red tape and unnecessary paperwork, when, in fact, it is a useful term to describe the systems and institutions that carry out the work of government. It is by no means a modern invention, either – as early as the 6th century BCE, Confucius proposed ways in which the business of the Chinese empire could be administered by a system of advisors to the emperor and a class of public servants.

Today, governments rely on a publicly funded civil service, composed of various government offices and departments, to provide an administrative system to manage the everyday business of the government, such as collecting taxes, and supplying and maintaining public goods and services. Civil servants are unelected and often specially trained for their work. In answer to the question 'who runs the country?', the answer is perhaps not obvious: while a government decides how it is run, it is the bureaucracy that actually manages it.

Non-governmental organizations

Not everything in a society is run by the government or its various bureaucratic departments. Certain elements are managed by independent organizations, which can range from small community groups to large international organizations. Some seek to influence government policy on specific issues, while others aim to complement public services, or provide them where governments do not. These non-governmental organizations (NGOs) are often charitable or non-profit-making organizations with altruistic aims and objectives. NGOs are less accountable than a similar governmental service, however, and the line between them and commercial organizations is not always clear. There are also organizations that are publicly funded to carry out some of the work of government departments, but not controlled directly by central government. Sometimes known as quasi-non-governmental organizations, or 'quangos', these include organizations constituted to do specific tasks, such as running prisons or overseeing the provision of public services.

Headquarters of the American Red Cross in Washington D.C.

Economic policy and taxation

In order to fund goods and services provided by the state, the people contribute financially through taxation. It is one of the major responsibilities of a government to determine the income and expenditure of the 'public purse', by deciding how much this contribution should be, how it should be raised and how it should be spent, and overseeing the management of its economic policy by the finance department or treasury.

Taxation can take several different forms, either as direct taxes on income or wealth, or as indirect tax on transactions, such as sales tax or value-added tax, and excise duty on goods. A government's economic policy, the way it balances its books between tax and public spending, is very much a reflection of its political ideology. Governments to the right of centre tend to minimize public spending, and so tax less and more indirectly than left-of-centre governments, to encourage the prosperity of businesses; left-leaning governments tend to have higher direct taxes to fund larger public expenditure.

SALE £ 30.00 S
30.00

OTTERBOX BLK IP6 1 @ £ 30.00
085033 £ 30.00

£ 0.00

Total
Debit Card: Visa
Capture Method: ICC

Change Due Trans Amt
£ 25.00

VAT Code
S 20%

VAT
£ 5.00

Welfare and social policy

Taxation was originally introduced to fund armed forces, at a time when perhaps the only responsibility of a monarch was the defence of the realm, requiring finance from a public treasury. Nowadays, however, a large proportion of public spending is to provide public goods and services, including transport and the utilities (although some of these, such as street lighting and rubbish collection, may be done at a local level), and social services, protecting the welfare of the people.

This social provision includes such things as healthcare, unemployment and sickness benefits, pensions and education, and the level to which it is funded from the public purse varies from one government to another. Those to the left of centre believe that welfare is a collective responsibility, to be wholly or partly funded by the state, with generous pensions and benefits as well as free or subsidized healthcare. More right-wing ideologies, however, advocate greater personal responsibility, through private insurance and pension schemes.

Constitutions and bills of rights

For a government to operate according to the principles of democracy, there must be a framework laid down by law, detailing the extent of its powers and how these are granted by the people. The idea of a written constitution was pioneered by the founders of the United States of America, and similar documents have accompanied the establishment of almost all democratic republics since the 18th century.

Among other things, a constitution describes the structure of government, the process by which it is elected, its period of office and the limits of its legislative power. In addition, it may describe the rights of citizens, or these may be additions or amendments to the constitution, or laid out in a separate bill of rights. There are even some democracies, notably Britain and Australia, that have no formal written constitution, but instead a combination of laws passed by parliament and legal precedents – judges' decisions – which together determine the way that government is constituted.

We the People

of the United States, in order to form a more perfect Union, establish Justice, insure domestic Tranquility, provide for the common defence, promote the general Welfare, and secure the Blessings of Liberty to ourselves and our Posterity, do ordain and establish this Constitution for the United States of America.

Article I

Section 1. All legislative Powers herein granted shall be vested in a Congress of the United States, which shall consist of a Senate and House of Representatives.

Section 2. The House of Representatives shall be composed of Members chosen every second Year by the People of the several States...

Section 3. The Senate of the United States shall be composed of two Senators from each State...

Section 4. The Times, Places and Manner of holding Elections for Senators and Representatives...

Section 5. Each House shall be the Judge of the Elections, Returns and Qualifications of its own Members...

Section 6. The Senators and Representatives shall receive a Compensation for their Services...

Laws and legislation

In power, a government puts its policies into practice through a system of legislation, making laws concerning taxation and expenditure, but also laws protecting the property, rights and freedoms of citizens. Many of these may already be laid down in a constitution or bill of rights, but through additional laws – and repealing or amendment of existing ones – a government can shape society to reflect its own philosophy.

Broadly speaking, governments can take either an authoritarian or a libertarian approach to law-making, prescribing codes of conduct or allowing a choice of lifestyle. This is most apparent in what is considered to be criminal behaviour – the things that are perceived as harmful to people's property, safety or moral welfare – and how people breaking these laws are punished. But governments can also exert influence through civil laws, those concerning such things as contracts and disputes, and the granting or removing of civil liberties.

Law and order

A number of institutions have been established to ensure that the laws of the land are observed, and that justice is done. These include a system of courts, a police force, and prison and probation services. Unlike other public institutions, however, they are generally independent and, though financed by the state, not directly controlled by the government. In this way, through a separation of powers (see page 128), the government is not above the law but subject to it, and the judiciary can act as a neutral arbiter.

Nevertheless, governments have considerable influence through the laws they make, and in particular the regulation of the legal system and the powers granted to the police. This varies according to the government's attitude to matters of public order. Policy can also determine recommendations for sentencing, such as the setting of fines, terms of imprisonment and even the imposition of capital punishment, as well as the balance between rehabilitation and punishment.

Defence and foreign policy

It is often argued that the first duty of a government is the protection of the state and its people. But defence against outside aggression is only one aspect of a government's relationships with other states. In addition to a department of defence, a government typically also has a department of foreign affairs that deals with matters of international trade, the movement of goods and labour, and economic, strategic and cultural links between countries.

This is complemented by a network of embassies and other outposts of the department of foreign affairs, based in other countries. Diplomatic staff are the frontline of communication with the governments of other countries. Foreign policy, especially the forging of military or economic alliances, is negotiated with the governments of other countries, and discussions between their respective ministers of foreign affairs or defence, or even the heads of state, either individually or at summit conferences (see page 364).

Armed forces and intelligence services

The armed forces form the most powerful, if not the most influential, of state institutions. Although publicly funded and under the control of the government through its department of defence, members of the forces often pledge their loyalty to their country or its head of state. And while their role is generally defined as defensive, they can also be deployed as an invading force by governments with expansionist ambitions or as the enforcers of an oppressive regime. Under more benign regimes, however, they often act simply as a deterrent force and also play a part in international relations, offering military assistance to allies, or contribute men and resources to international groups such as United Nations peace-keeping forces. In times of crisis, military forces are sometimes deployed to support the emergency services or, more controversially, to maintain public order. Complementing the armed forces are the intelligence services, whose role is primarily defensive, but increasingly with the rise of terrorism is directed at surveillance in the interests of national security.

Local and regional government

All but the smallest of nations have some system of local or regional government. These councils or regional authorities deal primarily with issues of purely local concern, such as responsibility for roads, street lighting, refuse collection and local amenities in general, or the local administration of services such as healthcare, education, police and fire services. Local authorities may be given some power to raise local taxes to fund these activities, or allocated a budget by central government, and their structure is often similar to central government in consisting of elected representatives and an unelected local bureaucracy.

A state may be divided into administrative districts in any of a number of ways: one tier of government may consist of regions such as counties, provinces or departments, and this may be subdivided to form another tier of government consisting of smaller rural and urban areas such as cities and towns, and even down to the level of individual villages and parishes.

The Hôtel de Ville in Paris houses the city's local administration.

Decentralization and devolution

The amount of power and responsibility given to local and regional government varies enormously from country to country. More libertarian political parties tend to advocate a minimal central government, and leaving local governments to manage their own affairs, but in practice often resist this decentralization once in power. Nevertheless, powers such as local administration, the raising of taxes and making laws are often granted to local authorities and, especially where there is a cultural or ethnic division of populations, a more full-blown devolution of power to regional parliaments or assemblies.

The power devolved to these local governments may not be a permanent arrangement, but if it is and offers real autonomy, it is akin to a federal state (see page 102). The United Kingdom, for example, is a unitary state that has devolved certain powers to regional parliaments, while the Kingdom of Belgium, with several distinct languages and communities, describes itself as a 'federal state composed of Communities and Regions'.

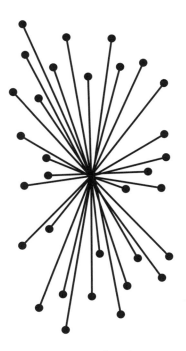

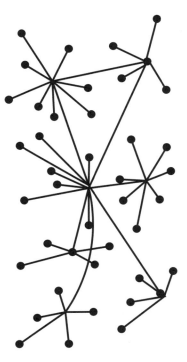

Centralized

Decentralized

Federalism

Some nations are formed of a federation of autonomous states. These have a central, federal government, which has powers to decide policy and make laws on national and international issues, and a number of regional governments at the state level that determine domestic policies and laws. One of the oldest federal states is Switzerland, which consists of 26 cantons covering 4 distinct cultural and linguistic regions, united as a confederation with a federal parliament. Other federal republics tend to be much larger countries with diverse regional populations, such as the United States, or the Russian Federation, which formed after the collapse of the USSR. Some politicians in Europe have pressed for increased federalism of the European Union giving stronger powers to a central government while retaining the autonomy of the separate member states. But many, while recognizing the benefits of intergovernmental cooperation for trade, have resisted the idea of increasing the power of supranational institutions fearing a loss of sovereignty and national identity.

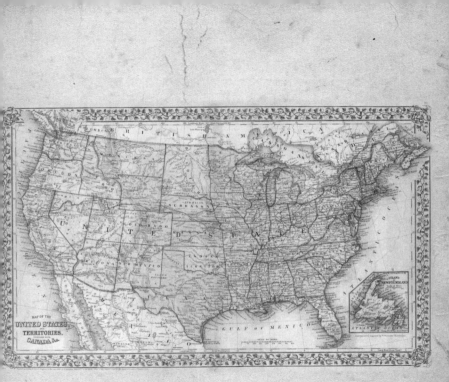

MAP OF THE
UNITED STATES,
TERRITORIES,
CANADA, &c.

Supranational institutions

Throughout the 20th century – especially in the periods following the two world wars – attempts were made to improve international relations by establishing international organizations that transcended national boundaries. Previously, international cooperation had relied on old imperial networks, or on alliances between countries for specific military or trade purposes. In the wake of the First World War, the League of Nations was set up with the aims of promoting peace and security, and at its peak had 58 member states. It was replaced after the Second World War by the United Nations, an intergovernmental organization with agencies including the United Nations Human Rights Council (UNHRC), United Nations Children's Fund (UNICEF), United Nations Educational, Scientific and Cultural Organization (UNESCO), World Health Organization (WHO) and International Labour Organization (ILO). Other important supranational organizations include the International Criminal Court, the Organization for Economic Cooperation and Development and the World Trade Organization (see page 386).

Democracy and democratic institutions

Winston Churchill famously quipped, 'Democracy is the worst form of government, except for all those other forms that have been tried from time to time.' Ideally, democracy is a system that enables citizens to decide the way in which their society is organized and governed, a government 'of, by and for the people', (see page 108) but how far modern forms of democracy have achieved this in practice is debatable, and varies from state to state.

The original Ancient Greek model of democracy, in which all eligible citizens participated directly in decision-making, would be impracticable in most societies, and so has been modified to a system of representatives elected by popular vote. The disadvantage, as some critics have pointed out, is that it runs the risk of merely legitimizing a small ruling elite. To minimize this risk, most democracies have strict and often complex legal frameworks based on a constitution, setting out the powers and limitations of governments and how they are elected.

Of, by and for the people

The idea that the people of a society should have the power to determine the way it is governed is the basis for all democratic systems. However, based on the wishes of the majority of the people, it may ignore or even contradict the wishes and rights of the minority, and may result in what Marx and Engels described as the 'dictatorship of the proletariat'. It could also be argued that the majority of people are not qualified to make important decisions of government.

Advocates of representative democracy counter that we can elect the most able to govern on our behalf. Power of government, although granted to a minority, can only be granted by the people, to whom those elected representatives are accountable. The British socialist politician Tony Benn neatly encapsulated the essence of representative democracy in five questions for those in power: What power have you got? Where did you get it from? In whose interest do you exercise it? To whom are you accountable? How can we get rid of you?

Suffrage

The cornerstone of modern democracy is the notion that citizens can participate in the political process by having the right to vote in elections. For modern democracies, this implies universal suffrage, giving all citizens over a certain age an equal vote. This has not always been the case – women were only reluctantly given the vote from the end of the 19th century, and eligibility for male voters has been conditional on status, education or property ownership. Nowadays, universal suffrage is taken to mean the enfranchising of every adult citizen, regardless of sex, social standing, religion or political persuasion. There are still, however, some who are legally excluded in many countries, including the insane and those serving prison sentences. Then there are those disenfranchised by the processes of registering their right to vote, which often exclude the disadvantaged, such as homeless, illiterate, disabled or unemployed people, or recent immigrants. Conversely, voting is seen in many places as a civic duty rather than a right and in some countries is compulsory.

Elections and representation

For a democracy to be a true reflection of the wishes of its citizens, there have to be regular opportunities for them to vote in elections. This is often enshrined in the constitution, which specifies either a fixed term of office for a national government, or at least a maximum length of time before an election is called. With regular national elections, perhaps every three or five years, the government is made accountable to the electorate. Typically, a country is divided into electoral districts or constituencies, which elect representatives to seats in a parliament or assembly for that term of office, but in some circumstances, such as the death of a representative, a local by-election will be held. Of course, citizens can be involved in political activity at any time, but it is only in these elections that the voter actually has a say in government. Increased use of referendums on constitutional or urgent matters, and the right for voters in an electoral district to call a vote of no confidence in an elected representative have been suggested as ways of improving voter involvement between elections.

Political parties

In representative democracies, any person who is eligible to vote is also eligible to stand for election, but few independent citizens do. Instead, candidates tend to have the backing of a political party, and are appointed or elected to stand by the party membership. The system of political parties has evolved around groups sharing distinct political ideologies, and their candidates stand on a 'platform' of their party's proposed policies. The number of seats won by each party nationally determines the ruling party. In states with only two major parties a simple majority decides which is government and which opposition, but alliances can be made to form a coalition government in parliaments and assemblies that contain a number of parties. What marks democracy from totalitarianism and dictatorship is the choice of views available to the electorate, and the freedom of political parties to represent this range of opinion. However, certain parties have been outlawed if they represent dangerously extremist views or have links with terrorist or criminal organizations.

Electoral systems

The process of electing representatives varies enormously from country to country. Some elections are for individual candidates on a 'first-past-the-post' basis, where the winner is simply the one with the most votes. But this can mean that minority parties never manage to gain an elected representative, despite having a proportion of popular support; and some candidates may be elected on substantially

less than 50 per cent of the vote, implying that more people voted against than for them. So more complex systems of proportional representation, reflecting voter preferences, have been devised – although they are not without their critics. The leaders of parties are generally chosen by the party membership, rather than the population as a whole. Voters vote for the party of their choice, and the leader of the winning party generally becomes the prime minister or leader of the legislature. Presidents are typically elected separately from the members of the legislature, either by a direct popular election or as in the USA indirectly by a system of electoral colleges.

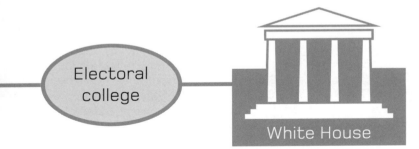

Presidential elections in the USA.

Republic

The term 'republic' can be used to describe any number of different types of state governed by elected leaders rather than a hereditary monarchy or dictatorship. As such, all republics are to a greater or lesser extent democratic states by definition. But not all democracies choose to call themselves 'republic', and many are at least nominally monarchies. Like democracy itself, republics have roots in the Ancient Greek and Roman states that for a time displaced the old kingdoms. Although some republican city-states were established in the Renaissance period, it wasn't until the late 18th century that absolute monarchies began to be replaced by national republics. Some 200 years later, they are the most common form of government. Some of the older nations retain royal families with no real political power alongside democratically elected parliaments in a 'constitutional monarchy'. One of the oldest of these, Britain, was for a time a republican-style 'Commonwealth', but actually restored its monarchy, albeit with greater powers retained by the Parliament.

Presidential government

Despite the almost universal rejection of absolute monarchy in favour of democracy, and antipathy to any form of tyrannical dictatorship, it seems that human nature favours some form of leadership. This is reflected in the models of representative democracy that have evolved, which almost invariably include the election of a single leader, such as a prime minister or president.

In a presidential system of government, the president is elected separately from the legislative body. Often this is a position of real power and responsibility, with the president acting as head of the executive branch of the government. As the chief executive, he or she plays an active role in the government of the country, often appointing ministers who similarly belong to the executive and oversee government departments. Some countries, however, have an essentially parliamentary system (see page 122), in which the president is an honorary head of state with little or no real power.

Parliamentary government

In many older democracies, the system of government evolved as power was gradually shifted from the monarchy to a parliament. Britain is the prime example of such a parliamentary government, which has served as a model for many other parliaments around the world. While a parliamentary democracy may have either a hereditary monarch or an elected president as nominal head of state, the executive power usually rests with a prime minister and cabinet or council of ministers, often referred to simply as 'the government', who are also members of the parliament.

In practice, the cabinet can only operate with the support of a majority of the parliament. The policy and decision-making of the cabinet of ministers requires the endorsement of parliament, without which it cannot pass laws. And, if the cabinet or prime minister no longer have the support of a majority of the parliament, there may be mechanisms allowing a vote of no confidence that can remove them from power.

Bicameral systems

The legislature or parliament in most democratic countries is divided into two houses, or chambers. The two-chamber, or bicameral, system evolved from the medieval European parliaments, which had separate assemblies for the aristocracy and the commoners. Some modern democracies still have unelected upper houses, with appointed or hereditary members, while presidential republics tend to have two houses with roughly equal powers but elected in different ways, such as the US Senate and House of Representatives.

The advantage of the bicameral system is in the enactment of laws, which requires the approval of both chambers. This helps to provide a moderating force of 'checks and balances' that prevent bad laws from being passed. Although bicameralism is widely considered an important feature of democratic government, there are some who point out that it often acts as an obstacle to radical legislation, and so can prevent necessary political reform.

President Obama addresses a joint session comprising both houses of the US Senate.

Cabinet

In parliamentary systems, the executive branch of government – the part that carries out the laws made by parliament – is overseen by ministers who together form a cabinet or council of ministers. The functions of the cabinet differ from country to country, ranging from a mainly advisory role to the head of government, to a policy- and decision-making group that effectively is the government.

Normally, ministers are appointed by the prime minister from the elected members of parliament, and given responsibility for different government departments. Among the most important members of the cabinet are the ministers for foreign and domestic affairs (known in the UK as Foreign and Home Secretaries), and the minister of finance (Chancellor of the Exchequer). In a presidential system, however, the ministers are not members of the legislative assembly. Lacking the same collective executive power, they act instead as advisors to the president, or as chief executives of their departments.

Separation of powers

An important principle of democracy is the clear distinction between different branches of government – the legislature, the executive and the judiciary – and the separation of their powers. If these institutions of government, each with specific responsibilities and powers, function independently no single branch can exercise absolute power. The role of the legislature is to make the laws, the executive to carry them out and the judiciary to decide when they have been broken.

The theory of separation of powers is most strictly adhered to in republics such as the USA, where the executive branch of government is identified with the president, the head of state, the legislature with the Senate and House of Representatives, and the judiciary with the courts. In practice, however, the three branches of government are interlinked in presidential governments, and are even more closely tied in parliamentary systems, where the prime minister and cabinet have executive power and are at the same time part of the legislature.

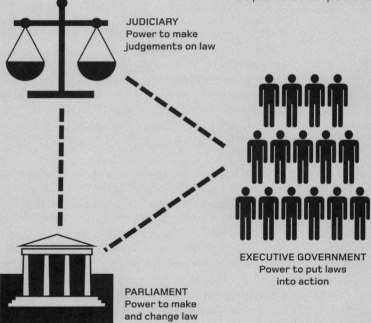

Separation of powers

JUDICIARY
Power to make
judgements on law

EXECUTIVE GOVERNMENT
Power to put laws
into action

PARLIAMENT
Power to make
and change law

Conservatism

A number of very different political ideologies have their roots in Enlightenment philosophy. It was a time of change, when thinkers suggested various alternatives to the old order, based on reason rather than faith. But there were those who resisted the idea of change, particularly the radical, tumultuous changes of the 18th century onwards.

Conservatives, as they came to be known, advocate a retention of traditional values, and tried and tested governmental structures, which they argue are the result of a long evolution. While conservatism takes several slightly different forms, conservatives in general tend to support the ideas of a ruling class or monarchy, traditional models of family and community, and a role for faith and religion in providing moral guidance and social cohesion. A central tenet is order, both in terms of an authoritarian attitude to public order and lawlessness, and in particular the protection of private property, and the belief in a hierarchical social order rather than equality.

Tradition

Conservatism as a political ideology emerged as a reaction to the profound political changes of the 18th century. And although it was seen as a counter-revolutionary movement at the time, and later as a moderating force, there is more to it than simply opposition to change. Central to the conservative philosophy is the idea that social and political structures have evolved gradually, and are the result of practical experience. Established traditions should be respected, as they contain the accumulated wisdom of complex societies.

These include institutions, such as organized religion and a ruling class, which form a solid basis for political systems and structures. There are also traditional social structures — families and communities — which are held together by shared beliefs and values, which tend to emphasize law and order, authority, conventional social behaviour and private property. Change to society and its organization, if at all necessary, should be gradual and cautious.

A ruling class, the right to rule

The counter-revolutionary aspect of conservatism was, unsurprisingly, especially prevalent in France, in the chaos following the Revolution. One of the founding fathers of European conservatism, Joseph de Maistre, pointed out what he saw as the disastrous effects of such a rapid and radical change in the political order, and especially the lack of a strong leader to maintain order. He believed that this was due mainly to the removal of the hereditary monarchy, whose authority came from long history of ruling and was endorsed by God.

While not all conservatives, especially today, are so supportive of royalty and their divine right to rule, the notion of a ruling class underlies all conservatism. Humans are not naturally equal, and the social order is based on a division between those who need to be led and those suited to lead. For many conservatives, this means a hereditary, privileged ruling class who are not only best qualified and experienced to rule, but will also protect the legacy of the country for the future.

Entitlement and property

Alongside the idea of a privileged class with a hereditary right – some would say duty – to rule, conservatism supports the idea of inheritance of wealth and property, and the ownership of private property in general. Entitlement is at the heart of this belief, harking back to the entitlement to property granted to noble families by the monarch in feudal systems. But starting with the rise of wealthy industrialists during the Industrial Revolution, the notion of entitlement evolved from divine rights and aristocracy to the protection of private property in a capitalist society.

Conservatism is now associated not so much with the old aristocracy as the new privileged class of industrialists and financiers, and their entitlement not only to wealth but also to a degree of power. Conservative governments, therefore, tend to shape their policies accordingly, placing more emphasis on protection of property than rights and freedoms, arguing that the creation of wealth benefits society as a whole.

Authoritarian conservatism

The conservative emphasis on protection of property, rather than individual rights and liberty, carries with it an implication that without strict laws and enforcement humans would revert to an anarchic state in which everybody would be out for what they could get. To maintain order and protect property governments must strictly exert their authority. This can be done by enforcing respect for traditional community and religious values, and obedience to political authority by reinforcing rigid social hierarchies.

Law and order are therefore a cornerstone of conservative policy, and in practice this may often be in the form of opposition to calls for civil rights and liberties, and even with some authoritarian conservatism an antipathy to popular participation in representative government. This sort of authority, wielded by a ruling elite both qualified and entitled to govern, places duty over rights, and is necessary to strengthen the institutions that maintain stability within society.

Paternalistic conservatism

Some conservatives believe in a paternalistic approach to government, which provides for the needs of the people rather than granting them rights or personal autonomy. In the conservative social hierarchy, the inferior classes are not only inherently lawless, but also in need of moral guidance and even material assistance, which is provided by the leadership of a superior, educated and wealthy class. This idea was prevalent in Victorian Britain and other industrialized countries, where philanthropy and public duty were held up as virtuous alternatives to socialist ideas. Paternalism, however, assumes that the government knows better than individuals what is good for them, and has the right to dictate how they should behave. It also assumes that the disadvantaged in society should be reliant on the goodwill of the wealthy ruling class. Contemporary conservatism continues this tradition with the idea of 'trickle-down' economics and moral guidance in the form of 'nudge' legislation – encouraging people to behave in 'good' ways, with tax breaks for savers and taxes on alcohol.

Are compulsory seatbelt laws an example of sensible legislation, or a case of 'nanny state' overprotection?

One-nation conservatism

A particular form of paternalistic conservatism emerged in Victorian Britain that stressed the traditional value of community and played down the authority of a ruling class. This was in response to liberal and socialist movements, which had demanded social change by highlighting inequalities in society. So-called 'one-nation' conservatism – the phrase coined by Prime Minister Benjamin Disraeli (pictured) – attempted to appeal to the inherent conservatism of the working class, and at the same time minimize the perception of an 'us and them' society. In contrast with the class struggle that had been proposed by Karl Marx (see page 196), one-nation conservatives interpreted the social hierarchy as an organic entity, with each of the social classes having obligations and duties to the others, and to society as a whole. The lower classes accept the obligation to provide their labour and forego some privileges, and in return the upper classes take on the duty of paternalistic care, reflected in a more progressive attitude to reform of social and welfare policy.

Christian democracy

In Europe and Latin America, the Catholic church, and to a lesser extent the Protestant churches of northern Europe, have long been a central pillar of community cohesion. Christian teachings have been influential in the social policies of conservative parties, tempering modern ideas of democracy with religious conservatism. A number of centre-right movements define themselves as Christian Democrats, adopting a generally liberal stance on economic policies, but a more traditional attitude towards social, cultural and particularly moral issues. Social conservatism is what marks European parties, such as the German Christian Democratic Union, from the left-of-centre social democrat parties. In Catholic countries, especially in Latin America, however, Christian Democracy tends to be much more right-wing on social issues. In the USA and Britain there is no formal link in the form of a specifically Christian Democrat party, and in strictly secular states such as France the movement is virtually non-existent.

Liberal and libertarian conservatism

Originally, in the 19th and early 20th century, 'liberal conservatism' referred to a combination of conservative social values – a respect for tradition, authority and religion – with a laissez-faire attitude to economics. This, said Edmund Burke, a founding figure of British conservatism, is a classically conservative stance: 'The laws of commerce are the laws of Nature, and therefore the laws of God.' As economic liberalism became part of the ideology of almost all mainstream conservatism, the word 'liberal' was increasingly dropped. It rose again in the mid-20th century, but this time it referred to the strand that adopted some measure of social (as opposed to economic) liberalism, moving somewhat to the left on issues such as welfare, civil rights and the environment. Confusingly, another strand of conservatism emerged, based on even stricter laissez-faire economic policies, and described as 'libertarian conservatism'. Advocating completely free and unregulated markets, libertarian conservatives are also socially right-wing, opposing redistribution of wealth through taxes.

The New Right

The term 'New Right' has been attached to a number of different conservative movements in the latter part of the 20th century. With the collapse of Soviet communism in the Warsaw Pact countries, it described the emergence of right-wing parties especially in eastern Europe. But it also refers to the development in the UK and USA in particular of a form of conservatism based not so much on class and tradition as a combination of very conservative social policies and very libertarian, laissez-faire economic policy.

A neoconservative movement – a backlash against the idealism of the 'swinging sixties' – flourished from the 1970s onwards, most influentially under the leadership of Margaret Thatcher in Britain and Ronald Reagan in the USA. In place of the paternalistic conservatism that preceded it, they advocated a meritocratic society with minimal government, opposed to government interference in the markets, and committed to cut both taxes and public spending.

Liberalism

The word 'liberal', with its connotations of freedom and generosity, has been used to describe a range of very different political ideologies. Used loosely, it has come to mean something similar to 'left-wing', especially in the USA, where it has even taken on a pejorative connotation. However in political theory, liberalism has a more precise meaning, referring to a philosophy based on principles of liberty and equality.

From its beginnings in the political philosophy of the Enlightenment period, liberalism has advocated ideas of democracy and civil rights, particularly for the individual, and developed into a movement supporting social reform. At the same time, a strand of economic liberalism has advocated free trade and minimal government interference. It is perhaps better then, rather than defining liberalism in terms of left or right, to see it as a broad range of social and economic stances that together sit at one end of a scale, the other end of which is occupied by authoritarianism.

Now in FULL colour

Liberal Democrat News

SPRING CONFERENCE EDITION

4 CHILDCARE
SUSAN KRAMER
on the Lib Dem proposals
going to Conference

5 GAZA
EDWARD DAVEY
and SARAH TEATHER
report on their visit

8 THE BACK PAGE
KIRSTY WILLIAMS
wants more powers
for the Welsh Assembly

Choose a better future

The individual

During the Renaissance, science and humanist philosophy began to challenge the authority of religion and hereditary privilege. This notion continued into the Enlightenment, when rational thought continued to replace faith and adherence to convention. The first politically liberal thinkers focused their attention on individuals as citizens of their societies, rather than their governments and leaders. And these individuals, especially in the fledgling democracies being established at the time, were citizens, not subjects.

Liberalism grew from the premise that individuals should have the opportunity to live their lives as they wish, and that government should enable them to do so, with minimal interference with their individual liberties. The supremacy of individual rights over state authority became the fundamental principle of classical liberalism, summed up in the dictum of the British 19th-century liberal philosopher John Stuart Mill: 'over his own body and mind, the individual is sovereign'.

Natural rights

An important element of liberalism is the emphasis on the rights of individuals to go about their lives freely. Traditionally, it had been thought that rights are divinely granted, and these were cited in defence of institutions, such as hereditary privilege and the power of the clergy, but during the Enlightenment philosophers such as John Locke (pictured) argued that there are some natural rights that are applicable to every human being. These, he said, are not only universal, but inalienable: they are not granted by a leader, government or religion, and do not depend on the beliefs and culture of a society, nor can they be restricted or removed by them.

These universal and inalienable natural rights to life, liberty and property are the foundations of the liberal ideology, and have been enshrined in the constitution of republics, such as the USA and France. They are, however, only the most basic of rights, which can be supplemented by legal rights granted to individuals by governments and legal systems.

Utilitarianism

One of the natural rights recognized by the US constitution, the right to 'pursuit of happiness', sounds a little curious to modern ears. But it reflects the concern of classical Greek philosophers with the pursuit of 'the good life', and moreover a contemporary notion that morality can be judged by the amount of happiness or harm caused by an action: its 'utility'. Utilitarianism was pioneered by the British philosopher Jeremy Bentham, who believed happiness is measurable, using a 'calculus of felicity'. The best course of action can be determined by the one that gives the greatest happiness to the greatest number of people. The concept of 'the greatest good' was further developed by John Stuart Mill, who more than Bentham saw its implications in terms of governments enabling citizens to pursue happiness. Mill also developed the idea of measuring happiness against harm, advocating laws that allow not only the greatest happiness of the greatest number, but also that cause least unhappiness, either by actual harm or restriction of liberty.

HAPPINESS   MISERY

British liberalism

Surrounded by the revolutionary atmosphere of the late 18th century, liberalism as a political movement flourished – perhaps surprisingly – in Britain. As well as the social liberalism built on Locke's championing of natural rights and Bentham's utilitarian moral philosophy, the Scottish political economist Adam Smith laid the foundations of liberal economic theory, based on the principles of the free market.

The most prominent British liberal thinker was undoubtedly J.S. Mill (pictured), whose 1859 book *On Liberty* set out the principles of liberalism in terms of 'the nature and limits of the power which can be legitimately exercised by society over the individual'. This introduced the concept of social liberty – freedom from the tyranny of political rulers, but also from the tyranny of the majority. Mill advocated that this could be achieved by establishing a number of civil and political rights, and a democratically elected government whose power is restricted by the requirement to recognize these rights.

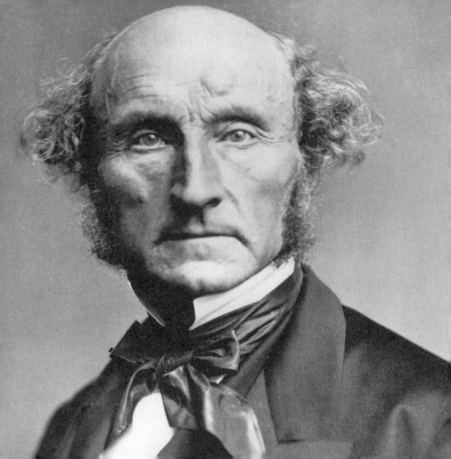

The harm principle

The fundamental principle of Mill's concept of liberalism was that every individual should have the liberty to live life as he or she pleases, without interference from others. But this principle raises a number of ethical questions, in particular in relation to the fact that allowing someone to do something may hurt other people, or restrict their freedom to do as they please. Mill suggested therefore that the individual's liberty should have its limitations when it harms others, and that it is the duty of society to prevent that harm.

He also recognized that some acts of omission – failing to do something that results in someone else's suffering – have the same effect. According to this 'harm principle', there is justification for some government regulation of the freedom to pursue happiness. But, as Mill pointed out, only to prevent harm to others – provided he or she is not being forced or tricked into doing something, the individual should be permitted to make decisions about his or her own well-being.

Toleration

Another cornerstone of liberalism is the concept of tolerance, that if someone is not actually harming anyone or interfering with their pursuit of happiness, they have the right to do as they please. Linked to this are specific liberties such as freedom of speech and of the press, and freedom of religion and political allegiance. The tolerant atmosphere in countries espousing these liberal principles, such as Britain and the USA in the 19th century, made them havens for refugees who were persecuted for their beliefs elsewhere. However, tolerance is now being tested in the multicultural societies that were created in part by such liberal acceptance, as some indigenous populations feel their way of life is threatened by immigration. Tolerance of freedom of speech and religion, too, is challenged by those who claim to be offended by opposing views. There is a difficult balance to be struck in our tolerance of religious or cultural customs that conflict with those of the wider society, such as arranged marriages or inhumane methods of animal slaughter.

US liberalism

Perhaps more than any other nation, the USA is founded on the principles of liberalism, with its commitment to equality and the inalienable rights to life, liberty and the pursuit of happiness. But 'liberalism' has in the USA taken on a variety of meanings since that declaration of independence. During the 19th and early 20th centuries, American liberalism was associated with the values of individualism, independence and self-responsibility that had become 'the American Way', with a dislike of too much government interference, especially in economic matters. Classical liberalism's emphasis on self-reliance meant an opposition to government spending on welfare, but the Great Depression of the 1930s forced liberals to soften their stance on social policy. F.D. Roosevelt's New Deal marked the beginning of a new kind of US liberalism, with increased government involvement in both social and economic matters. This strand of progressive liberalism continues to the present in the policies of the Democratic party, contrasted with the conservatism of the Republicans.

Small government

While in Europe liberalism was increasingly influenced by socialist ideas, especially in areas of welfare, public health and education, American liberalism stuck more to the classical principle of minimal government authority over the freedom of the individual. This American attitude was summed up by the writer Henry David Thoreau: 'government is best which governs least'. Classical liberalism considered government as something of a necessary evil, and laws and regulation as obstacles to personal liberty and, above all, free enterprise.

The notion of small government persisted in the 20th century, in the form of an opposition to the rising tide of socialism. This interpretation of liberalism, with the emphasis on small government, deregulation of commerce and minimum public spending rather than individual liberty and equality, developed from the free-market capitalism espoused by 19th-century liberals. Now it is the orthodoxy not of the progressive liberals, but the socially and economically right-wing conservatives.

Constitutionalism

Liberalism as a political movement began with the ideas of John Locke, and was first put into practical form by the founding fathers of the US republic in their Declaration of Independence. They realized that liberty and rights were closely linked to limiting by law the powers of any government. A government would only be considered legitimate if it remained within the legal limitations, which they set out in a constitution.

Constitutionalism is the belief that a government's authority derives from the constitution. This belief is, however, not as simple as it seems: the laws limiting government are themselves created by government. The implication is that the constitution represents a higher authority than that of the government, and the limitations on governmental power must be so entrenched that they are resistant to change or repeal, and enshrined in a written constitution. That is not to say that the 'higher law' of the constitution is fixed, but that changes to it cannot be made lightly.

Liberal democracy

The basic principles of liberalism – protection of individual rights of liberty and protection against oppressive government – have been so widely accepted that they are sometimes seen as synonymous with the idea of democracy. Although democracies may take on a variety of forms (see page 106), today most describe themselves as liberal democracies in that they combine the democratic principle of fair and free elections with the liberal principle of protection of rights and freedoms. However, in practice, democracies can and do limit certain freedoms, and many governments in so-called liberal democracies impose regulations on trade and industry, and the free movement of labour, and control the distribution of wealth through systems of taxation. In addition, they may take an active role in social policy. The justification for this type of intervention is typically that it is sometimes necessary to become less liberal in order to be more democratic; that restrictions and regulation may be needed to protect certain basic freedoms, and even democracy itself.

Social Darwinism

Charles Darwin's theory of evolution, proposed in his 1859 book *On the Origin of Species*, gave rise to a number of theories of society in the late 19th century, linking the idea of 'the survival of the fittest' to liberal political ideology. This social Darwinism, as it became known, argued that the strongest and richest sections of society should be allowed to prosper without restriction by government regulation, and that protection of the weak and poor through welfare programmes and redistribution of wealth runs counter to the evolution of a healthy and prosperous society. This provided a rationale for small government and minimal social spending, and in particular for a laissez-faire approach to competitive capitalism. The idea of allowing unproductive sections of society to die out, enabling the strong to prosper, was rejected by mainstream liberals as aggressive individualism. However, some vestiges of the concept can be seen in classical liberal policies, such as the encouragement of successful enterprise to promote economic growth and opposition to a socialized welfare state.

English classical liberal political theorist Herbert Spencer (1820–1903) is today best known as the author of the expression 'survival of the fittest'.

Social liberalism

J.S. Mill, one of the greatest advocates of liberal ideology, initially advocated government only to protect those rights, and believed in an unregulated free-market economy without the burden of excessive taxation. But he later came to recognize that individual freedom is not incompatible with the good of the community and liberalism should also concern itself with social justice. Persuaded by what he saw as social injustices in Victorian Britain, he proposed that government economic policy should aim to mitigate poverty, and have a role in public health and education. This strand of British liberalism gained support, leading to radical social welfare programmes and unprecedented progressive taxation, introduced at the beginning of the 20th century by liberal governments. These paved the way for a comprehensive welfare state in the UK after the Second World War. And it was an English liberal economist, John Maynard Keynes, who provided President F.D. Roosevelt with the framework for his New Deal, bringing social liberalism to the USA in response to the Great Depression.

The crisis triggered by the Great Depression and Dust Bowl of the 1930s plunged many Americans into poverty—a crisis that was finally remedied with the introduction of the New Deal.

The 'invisible hand'

During the Enlightenment, a sea change in the approach to 'political economy' provided the basis for liberal economic thinking. In 1776, Adam Smith published *The Wealth of Nations*, which laid the foundations for modern economics, and provided the rationale for an economic model that has been at the heart of liberal democracies ever since. Smith argued that people are rational and act in their own interests if left to their own devices. In commerce, their actions are influenced by the laws of supply and demand; order and equilibrium is maintained by the 'invisible hand' of a free and open market.

Smith asserted that if business is left to operate in a free market, individuals and firms work to their mutual benefit and ultimately for the good of all. The idea that a market economy, free of restriction by government, would bring stability and prosperity to the community as a whole fitted ideally with liberal philosophy, and has figured in all forms of liberal economic policy.

Economic liberalism

Economic liberalism, the belief in a capitalist market economy and private ownership of the means of production, is contrasted with social liberalism (see page 174), and the two are sometimes awkward to reconcile. But while classical liberalism, and later neoliberalism (see page 180), have strictly applied the principles of free-market economics, there has always been a strand of liberalism that concedes there is a place for some government intervention and regulation of commerce, and that certain public goods and services are legitimately the responsibility of the state.

A commitment to free trade and open competition, for example, does not preclude regulation to prevent monopolies, or tariffs to control competition from other countries. Even in the most liberalized economies, trade is never entirely free – copyright and patent laws, immigration control and taxes all place some restrictions on the markets, and government subsidies and even bailouts give some firms a competitive advantage.

Neoliberalism

By the mid-20th century, liberalism had evolved from its classical roots of minimal government power over the rights of the individual and minimal intervention in economic affairs, to the social liberalism of a market economy guided and regulated by the state protecting the welfare as well as the rights of its citizens. But a number of economists, notably Friedrich Hayek and Milton Friedman, advocated a much more laissez-faire attitude to economic policy, termed 'neoliberalism'.

These ideas were aggressively enforced by the dictator Augusto Pinochet in Chile during the 1970s, but gained respectability when this economic liberalization was adopted in the USA and Britain by Ronald Reagan and Margaret Thatcher. In essence, it was a reversal of the trend towards social liberalism, and instead a strengthening of the free markets, through a programme of reduction in government spending, especially social spending, lowering of taxation, deregulation of business and banking, and extensive privatization.

Privatization

A central concept of liberalism in all its forms has been the limitation of government's powers to what is necessary and good for society as a whole. Classical liberals argued that government should be confined to defence, administration of justice and public works. As social liberalism replaced classical liberalism, the understanding of what constitutes 'public works' expanded – in addition to defence and justice, liberal governments considered social issues to be the responsibility of the public sector, and even utilities such as water, gas and electricity, and public transport. In the 1980s, however, neoliberal economists argued that public ownership led to inefficiency, and many Western governments began the process of returning these businesses to the private sector. Since then, many European countries have not only reversed the public ownership of utilities, but also privatized traditionally national industries and services, such as post offices, and outsourced the work of government departments, such as prison services, tax collection and policing, to private firms.

In Europe, many railways started out as private enterprises, were later nationalized, and have more recently been privatized once again.

Socialism and communism

Socialism and communism are two interconnected, and often confused, political ideas. Communism is, broadly speaking, a political ideology or philosophy, whereas socialism is primarily the socioeconomic system associated with it. Like many modern political ideologies, communism has its beginnings in the Enlightenment, and developed in opposition to the rise of capitalism in the Industrial Revolution. In the mid-19th century, Karl Marx presented a comprehensive case for communist politics and socialist economics, in which the means of production, distribution and exchange are owned or controlled collectively.

The political implications of this economic system are social justice, equality and cooperation, in contrast to the liberal emphasis on freedoms and individual rights. There have been numerous interpretations of socialism since Marx, with some arguing for a workers' revolution to end the capitalist system, and others for more gradual democratic reform.

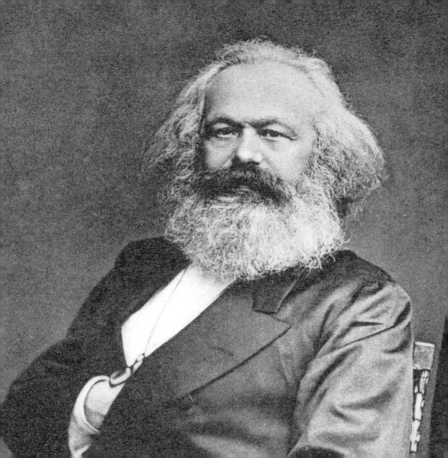

Equality

Common to all varieties of socialism and communism is the notion of equality and fairness, and especially an equitable distribution of wealth. The socialist economic model is based on transferring the means of production from private hands to a collective ownership, so that no one has more than their fair share of the fruits of that production. This idea was encapsulated in the maxim adopted by Karl Marx: 'From each according to his ability, to each according to his need.'

As with so many principles, the notion of fair distribution has been interpreted in different ways. In order to achieve the objective of a socialist state, production needs to be encouraged by rewarding the workers by sharing the wealth 'according to deeds' – in proportion to the amount and quality of their contribution to it – but the aim is ultimately to produce enough to distribute production according to need, even if someone is unable to contribute to the production, and so provide for the disadvantaged in society.

From each according to his ability, to each according to his need.

Rousseau: the general will

In the Enlightenment period, political philosophers proposed freedom and equality as the foundations for modern society in place of the old order of monarchs and subjects. Jean-Jacques Rousseau, however, saw things from a different perspective. In his view, civil society does not promote freedom and equality, as it is designed to protect private property rather than rights and liberty. Because of this it actually creates inequality. Left to their own devices, people in a 'state of nature' are free, but become enslaved by the restrictions of society. For them to become free again, they must act and make decisions collectively, so that individuals submit to the 'general will' of the people. This depends on each member of society being equal in status, which cannot be achieved until they also abandon their right to private property and treat resources as being available for all. Writing in the mid-18th century, Rousseau anticipated the basic elements of socialism that emerged with industrialization and the inequalities created by capitalist ownership of mills and factories.

18th- and 19th-century revolutions

Socialism, and especially communism, are frequently associated with the idea of revolution – not necessarily sudden and violent uprisings, but certainly radical social and economic change. At the end of the 18th century, the American Revolution embodied the idea of liberty and rights that were the foundation of liberalism, but in the French Revolution (maybe because of Rousseau's influence) the rallying cry was *'Liberté, égalité, fraternité'*, placing the emphasis more on equality and collectivity.

Socialism and communism emerged in Europe against a backdrop of revolutions in 1848. It is no coincidence that the *Communist Manifesto* was written in the same year, and not long after, in 1871, the first truly socialist revolution took place in France, establishing a revolutionary socialist government, the Paris Commune. The Commune was described at the time by Karl Marx as a model for revolutionary government, and inspired a number of similar uprisings in France and elsewhere.

Barricades around French government buildings during the Paris Commune.

Utopian socialism

The socialist goals of an egalitarian and cooperative society have often been dismissed by critics as naive and unrealistic, and many early socialist thinkers were labelled 'utopian'. Among them were the French political and economic philosopher Henri de Saint-Simon and the Welsh reformer Robert Owen, whose visions of an ideal modern society based on cooperation and equality were an inspiration to more realistic socialist theorists including Karl Marx.

Unlike later socialists, utopian socialists did not advocate political revolution or conflict between capitalists and workers. Owen, as a factory owner, was in a position to put his ideas into practice, and set up just such a community in a mill in New Lanark, Scotland, and later planned a larger one in the USA. Utopian socialism was short-lived, however, as revolutionary communist ideas offered a better chance of bringing about social change. However, some of the principles of utopianism were taken up by parts of the growing anarchist movement.

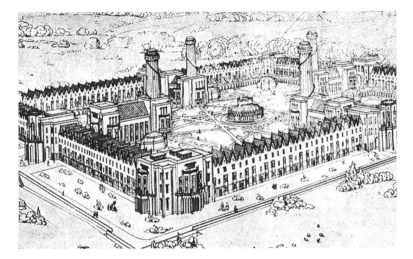

Robert Owen's vision of New Harmony, a short-lived but influential utopian settlement established in Indiana, USA in 1825.

Community, cooperation and common ownership

One element of utopian socialism that found an early application was the idea of collectivism – communities collectively taking responsibility for production of goods and service, and their distribution. While the idea is common to all strands of socialist thinking, it has also operated successfully within capitalist societies. The idea of was pioneered by the cooperative movement of Rochdale, in north England, in the 19th century, and continues in many countries today.

Quite separate from government, cooperatives are autonomous not-for-profit businesses or organizations owned and managed by their members for their mutual benefit. The best known are consumer cooperatives – the collectively owned and run retail outlets and chains – and cooperative insurance services, but there are also workers' and housing cooperatives, and credit unions that provide for the needs of the community. While not formally aligned with any political ideology, the movement is an example of the socioeconomic principle of socialism in practice.

The original cooperative store in Rochdale is now a museum.

Marx: philosophy, history

Karl Marx was undoubtedly the most influential socialist thinker of all time, and his ideas laid the foundations for modern socialism and communism. As a student in Berlin, he came across the ideas of Georg Hegel, who believed that history can be seen as a process with a discernible structure: each period has defining characteristics, which he called the *Zeitgeist*: the spirit of the age. Every idea has a contradictory idea ('thesis' and 'antithesis'), and the tension between the two creates a new notion – the synthesis – which forms the spirit of the age that follows.

This appealed to Marx, but as a down-to-earth materialist and atheist, he rejected the philosopher's preoccupation with metaphysics. Marx adapted Hegel's dialectic – of thesis–antithesis–synthesis – to show how social, economic and political ideas progressed one to another. At the heart of his thinking was the notion that material conditions such as the means of production brought about social and economic change.

The Dialectic

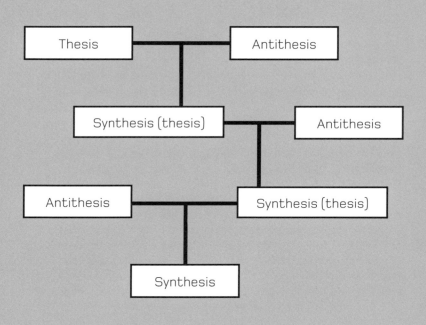

Marx: economics, analysis of capitalism

As well as being a philosopher and historian, Marx was an economist and, having recognized the dominance of the capitalist system, set out to make a thorough analysis of it in *Das Kapital*. Marx believed that capitalism could be a force for progress as it encouraged economic growth and technical innovation, but also created social injustice and was inherently unstable. In his analysis, however, he saw capitalism as just another stage in human history – the synthesis of conflict between serfs and nobles in a basically agricultural society, which had been brought about by the material change of industrialization. With capitalism, the means of production now rested in the hands of the factory and mill owners, the 'bourgeoisie', who exploited the labour of the working class, the 'proletariat'. Capitalism, he explained, had now produced the conditions for change to the next stage of historical development through the tension between these two classes, which would result in conflict, triggered by financial instability and increasing social unrest.

Das Kapital.

Kritik der politischen Oekonomie.

Von

Karl Marx.

———

Erster Band.

Buch I: Der Produktionsprocess des Kapitals.

Class struggle

Central to Marx's theories of socialism and communism was the concept of tension and conflict between classes, and in his analysis, the history of all hitherto existing societies is the history of class struggle. His interpretation of the progression of history was based on the dialectic: two contradictory concepts in conflict resulting in a third, new idea.

In the ancient world, Marx argued, the conflict was between masters and slaves, which was resolved by the creation of a feudal system. This in turn produced a class of nobility opposed by a class of serfs, and the conflict between them, with industrialization as its catalyst, created capitalism. Under capitalism the class struggle is between bourgeoisie and proletariat, and Marx proposed that the synthesis of this conflict, communism, can be brought about by working-class realization of their situation. The *Communist Manifesto* ends with a call for greater class consciousness, and for the proletariat to use the class struggle as a tool for change.

Marx: politics and the inevitability of socialism

Before writing his massive book, *Das Kapital*, Marx had been a co-author with Friedrich Engels of the *Communist Manifesto*, in which he explains that capitalism contains within it the seeds of its own destruction. Because capitalism has created two classes, the business-owning bourgeoisie and the labouring proletariat, the tension between them will inevitably result in social and economic change. In the words of the Manifesto, 'What the bourgeoisie produces above all is its own grave diggers', meaning that capitalism has created the conditions for a conflict in which the proletariat will seize ownership of the means of production, and change the 'dictatorship of the bourgeoisie' to a 'dictatorship of the proletariat' run on socialist economic and social principles. But this is, Marx says, only a transitional stage to the ultimate conclusion of historical development, communism – a classless society that brings to an end the historical conflict between classes, and in which private property and the state itself no longer exist.

Manifest

der

Kommunistischen Partei.

———

Veröffentlicht im Februar 1848.

Neo-Marxism

The term 'neo-Marxism' is used to describe a number of different movements that arose in the middle of the 20th century, which re-examined Marxism in the light of modern developments and introduced ideas from other disciplines. Disillusion with the way that communism had turned out in practice in the Soviet Union had prompted a reappraisal of Marxist ideas as early as the 1930s, notably by the group known as the Frankfurt School in Germany. Based originally in the Institute for Social Research, this group incorporated elements of sociology and psychology into traditional Marxist theory, while playing down the emphasis on class struggle. In Italy, Antonio Gramsci suggested that economic and class issues, although important, are not the sole motivators of social revolution and that capitalism maintained its power through cultural hegemony, making change seem unthinkable. These neo-Marxist ideas were taken up after the Second World War by theorists such as Michel Foucault in France and the so-called New Left in the USA and Britain.

The New Left

Several of the so-called Frankfurt School of neo-Marxists settled in the USA, including Herbert Marcuse (pictured), whose ideas became the foundation for the New Left movement in the 1960s and 1970s. Closely associated with student protest movements, the New Left was less concerned with traditional left-wing issues, such as class struggle and workers' revolution, and placed more emphasis on social reform.

The New Left movement was taken more seriously in Britain, led as it was by respected Marxist academics who departed from the strict Marxist/Leninist line of the ailing Communist Party of Great Britain – adopting the American emphasis on social reform, while retaining Marx's notion of class struggle. The popularity of the New Left waned in the 1980s, but some elements of new-left thinking have re-emerged recently in, for example, Spain and Greece, where Podemos and Syriza have abandoned the 'old left' traditional socialist and communist parties in their opposition to capitalism.

State ownership and nationalization

One of the defining features of the socialist socio-economic model is that the means of production and distribution are owned and controlled by the people rather than privately. This can be done by cooperatives at a community level, where all members have a stake in the business, and goods and services are produced for their benefit rather than profit. Many socialists also advocate state ownership of industries, so that they belong to the people of a nation as a whole, with authoritarian communist states taking all businesses into state ownership, effectively running state monopolies in every industry. Other countries have adopted the idea of the state-owned enterprise (SOE) to a greater or lesser extent, having a mix of private and nationalized companies, which may or may not be in competition. SOEs formed a significant proportion of many countries' economies during the 20th century, particularly those under social-democratic governments, but as laissez-faire free-market policies became more widespread from the 1980s, many were taken back into private ownership.

Central economic planning

Nationalized industries are a way for people to own the means of production and distribution. In this form of state socialism, the state owns the firms and makes decisions about how much should be produced and how it should be distributed. This, in turn, means that the entire economy can be centrally planned by the government. With no competitive market determining prices the government can decide directly on the allocation of resources.

And because the goods are produced for use rather than profit, production does not have to react to market fluctuations and the output can be planned so that there is no surplus or deficit – effectively ironing out the ups and downs of the business cycle and bringing stability of prices and employment. In practice, however, a nation's economy is too large and complex for any single organization to manage, and communist states that attempted central economic planning have often failed to meet the needs of the people.

Revolutionary socialism

Marx developed his influential theories in a period of history shaped by revolutions – social, cultural, industrial and economic. However, other than the short-lived Paris Commune of 1871, no revolution succeeded in his lifetime to replace capitalism with socialism. But his ideas were vindicated in the 20th century, when Vladimir Lenin and Leon Trotsky led the Russian workers into revolution and established a socialist state. They believed this could not have happened without a vanguard of revolutionary socialists to help the proletariat to achieve class consciousness and mobilize them into action. Although Marx and his fellow revolutionary socialists advocated revolution, they did not necessarily mean the sort of hard-fought and bloody battle of the Russian Revolution. Rather, they refer to a rapid removal of capitalism and the bourgeoisie, and complete social and economic transformation. In practice, however, this usually involves the use of force, and far from being a swift overthrow of capitalism, is often a protracted armed struggle against the forces of the establishment.

Revisionism

There are perhaps more divisions and different ideological interpretations in socialism and communism than any other political philosophy. Many of the older-established communist groups believe that only they are true to the fundamental principles of socialism and communism, and often reject any watering down of what they see as orthodoxy. New ideas are often dismissed as 'revisionist', a pejorative term that is used to refer to any of the many reinterpretations of Marx's original communist theory.

The first major split in the movement came with reformist evolutionary socialism, which was seen as revisionist by revolutionaries, such as Rosa Luxemburg, and later was at the core of the split between Lenin (revisionist) and Trotsky (old guard, pictured). Later, the argument between fundamentalists and revisionists was not over the means of achieving socialism, but the ends: orthodox Marxism views as revisionist any idea that does not see as its goal the overthrow of capitalism.

Reformism, or evolutionary socialism

Instead of sudden, radical changes, a number of socialists proposed a more gradual transition or evolution. The idea of evolutionary socialism was first formulated around the turn of the 20th century by a German socialist, Eduard Bernstein. He suggested that socialism could be achieved by democratic means, by reforms introduced through parliament and the existing political system. Reformism was rejected by orthodox revolutionary socialists, such as Rosa Luxemburg, who not only saw it as ineffective, but were also impatient for change.

However, the reformist idea of alleviating the injustices of capitalism, and in time replacing it entirely, became the guiding principle of several democratic socialist parties in Europe, including Bernstein's German Social Democratic Party (SPD). In the end, the critics were proved right, and evolutionary socialism did not bring about a socialist state – in fact in 1959, the SPD officially changed its policy to one of social reform rather than working towards an end to capitalism.

Alexis Tsipras led the anti-austerity party SYRIZA to victory in the Greek general election of 2015.

Communism

A common misconception, particularly among those critical of communism, is that 'communism' refers to the political and economic system seen in self-styled 'communist states', such as Soviet Russia. These states, however, are very different from communism as it was envisaged by Marx. Despite the label 'Marxist–Leninist' they had little in common with either Marx or Lenin, and more to do with the authoritarian rule of Stalin, which many true communists regard as a form of state capitalism.

In contrast, the communism described by Marx and Engels in the *Communist Manifesto* is the final stage of a historical development, which is realized once a socialist state has been established, and the working class has gained control of the means of production. Once it has been achieved, true communism can be brought about – in Marx's words 'characterized by the absence of social classes, money and the state'. A far cry from any so-called communist state ever established.

Libertarian socialism

Within the socialist movement there are several different and often opposing views. There is, for example, the divergence of opinion between revolutionary and reformist socialism. And there are also those who reject the idea of state socialism and state ownership, which they see as creating a new, oppressive political and economic elite, little better than capitalism. These libertarian socialists call for an end to centralized control over the means of production, giving workers control of their own workplace through trades unions and workers' councils, and introducing direct democracy in decentralized political government. Libertarian socialism is directly opposed to any authoritarian institutions, including the state, making its core philosophy very close to that of anarchism and, in particular, anarcho-syndicalism (see page 238). But where anarcho-syndicalists see the absence of the state as a necessary condition for achieving a libertarian socialism, libertarian socialists see the eventual disappearance of the state as a result of applying socialist principles.

Trades unions and the labour movement

Industrialization not only changed the pattern of peoples' working lives, moving them from agricultural jobs or traditional crafts to factories and mills in the cities, but it also changed who they worked for and their job security. In the 19th century, workers in newly industrialized countries began to form trade unions (also known as labour unions) – associations with the aim of maintaining or improving the conditions of their employment, filling a gap left by the old craftsmens' guilds.

While this was generally a practical rather than a political movement, dealing with negotiation of wages and conditions of employment and so on, it, perhaps inevitably, evolved a strong socialist undercurrent. This, after all, was a prime example of the workers of the world uniting and acting collectively to ensure the value of their labour-power was reflected in their pay packets. More than this, trades unions helped to instil a sense of class consciousness and, because of this, the movement became a significant force for socialism.

Social democracy

From the evolutionary socialism of reformists such as Bernstein (see page 216) emerged a movement that sought not to overthrow the capitalist system but to combine it with socialist policies to remove its injustices and inequalities. Rather than whole-scale state socialism, social democrats advocated state ownership of certain businesses, such as those providing public goods and services, and partially owning others in key industries. Other firms, although in private ownership, would be managed jointly by the shareholders and workers, and their operations strictly regulated by the government. A redistribution of wealth from rich to poor is achieved in social democracy through taxation, with the money raised being used to provide public services, subsidize state-owned enterprises and make welfare payments. Although rejected by both hardline communists and capitalists, the mixture of socialist and capitalist ideologies had great appeal, and social democrat parties of various sorts have been formed in most European countries.

The 'Third Way'

In the years immediately following the Second World War, people in West Germany were faced with the prospect of rebuilding their country. They found themselves, literally, between two opposing political ideologies, communism and capitalism, but chose what became known as the 'Third Way', an attempt to reconcile the two. In essence this was an adoption of capitalist economic policies alongside mainly socialist social policies, a concept known as the social market economy.

Unlike social democrats, third-way adherents put an emphasis on minimal government interference in industry and commerce, preferring partnerships between public and private owners. Rather than redistribution of wealth, they recommended greater equality of opportunity. The so-called 'economic miracle' of post-war Germany was attributed to the policies of the Third Way, inspiring other countries to adopt a similar approach. It loomed large in European politics and paved the way for the more laissez-faire capitalism of the 1980s.

Communitarianism

Socialism's emphasis on collectivity contrasts starkly with classical liberalism's focus on the individual, encapsulated in Margaret Thatcher's 1987 statement 'There is no such thing as society.' Many on the right-wing, although supporting capitalist principles, are uncomfortable with the loss of community values that neoliberal policies have brought along with them. Communitarianism, although not a political movement as such, has become a principle informing the policies of many centrist governments in recent years. Communitarians believe that as well as the right's dismissal of collectivity, there has been a failure of the left to recognize traditional culture and community, and that these should be revived by strengthening civil society. Rather than either the individual or the state being responsible for social welfare, it should be communities, using what communitarians describe as 'social capital'. Described by its advocates as a sort of 'radical centrism', communitarianism has its greatest support in countries that have enthusiastically pursued neoliberal policies, such as the USA and Britain.

Anarchism

The roots of the word 'anarchism' lie in the Greek *anarchos*, meaning 'without a ruler'. It is a political doctrine that seeks radical social change, particularly the replacement of the state with some form of non-government, non-hierarchical voluntary cooperation between free individuals, sometimes described as mutual aid. With many different schools, ranging from collectivism to libertarian individualism, anarchism can be difficult to place on the political spectrum. It is usually described as a radical left movement. Though ideas of ruler-less societies stretch back to classical antiquity, anarchism as a visible movement emerged in the mid-19th century, its theoretical roots being planted by Pierre-Joseph Proudhon who stated, 'As man seeks justice in equality, so society seeks order in anarchy.' Anarchism spread worldwide during the early 20th century, particularly in Spain. Quashed during the Spanish Civil War, anarchism re-emerged with the 1968 student rebellions. Today its ideas and practice influence anti-capitalist, anti-war and anti-globalization protests.

Anti-statism

Opposition to the state, or anti-statism, is fundamental to all forms of anarchism and is a key element distinguishing it from Marxism and socialism. For anarchists, the state in all its forms – governments, authority, hierarchical and power structures – is the enemy. It is harmful because it controls people's lives, and unnecessary because people are capable of governing themselves. Anarchists seek to abolish the state, an aim that applies not only to authoritarian regimes but also to representative democracies.

Anarchists do not want to take over the state; they want to abolish it. They eschew the parliamentary process, they do not support or form political parties and refuse to vote on the grounds that by doing so they contribute to the very system they oppose. Like Marxists they seek social revolution and have long been linked with working-class action, but they oppose the socialist model, which they regard as the dictatorship of the proletariat, merely exchanging one power structure for another.

Henry David Thoreau (1817–1862) wrote 'that government is best which governs not at all'. This entails a rejection of all authority and political structures.

Utopianism

Anarchists believe humans are capable of governing themselves and do not need hierarchical power structures, whether church, state or monarchies. Free from the shackles of authority, a natural social order will emerge that creates its own rules based on social justice, cooperative work and mutual aid. Many believe this is unrealistic and anarchists have been accused of being utopian. However, the Anarchist Federation make the point that an anarchist utopia would not be a heavenly vision or a return to a golden age, but a world in which violence, exploitation and oppression have disappeared.

Since the 19th century there have been a number of significant radical utopian or communitarian anarchist communities, including New Lanark in the UK and New Harmony in the USA, both set up by industrialist Robert Owen. Brook Farm in the USA was inhabited by, among others, Ralph Waldo Emerson and Henry David Thoreau, while the Whiteway Colony in the UK was founded by followers of Leo Tolstoy's Christian anarchism.

Sieben Linden is a self-governing, self-sufficient ecovillage in the Altmark of Germany.

Individualist anarchism

Individualist anarchism puts personal freedom and the rights of the individual above the authority of the state, nation, class or any hierarchical structure. The earliest strand of anarchism, it is in effect an assertion of individual sovereignty. William Godwin, the first to develop what is known as philosophical anarchism, was an early influence. He argued that government corrupts society, because it encourages dependency and ignorance, and imposes upon an individual's right to 'private judgement'. Godwin also dismissed various cooperative and rule-determined practices, such as law, private property and marriage, as mental enslavement. Subsequently, Max Stirner promoted a more extreme view arguing for what he described as unions of 'egoists', based entirely on self-interest. As individualist anarchism spread, Benjamin Tucker suggested each individual should enjoy the maximum liberty, compatible with others. Individualist anarchists tend to reject revolution as a means of bringing about change, arguing that it can result in new hierarchies.

Liberty

NOT THE DAUGHTER BUT THE MOTHER OF ORDER

Vol. III.—No. 15.   BOSTON, MASS., SATURDAY, OCTOBER 3, 1885.   Whole No. 67.

"For always in thine eyes, O Liberty!
Shines that high light whereby the world is saved,
And though thou slay us, we will trust in thee."

                         John Hay.

PRIEST — KING — BURGHER — SERF.

I.

PRIEST—AGE OF GREGORY VII.

Kneel! Henry, kneel! Strip off thy coat of mail,
In penitential garment kiss the feet

Hypocrisy.

To the Editor of Liberty:

There is great temptation for lucid men of principle to anathematize those who make a profession.

Judges the Dangerous Criminals.

[Ed. W. Chamberlain in John Swinton's Paper.]

I have in my possession the deposition of Ambrose H. Purdy, who for eight years acted as public prosecutor in the United States Circuit Court in New York city, where Judge Benedict, during that time, presided. Mr. Purdy testifies:

Published between 1881 and 1908 by Benjamin Tucker, *Liberty* was an American anarchist periodical.

Anarcho-syndicalism

One of the better-known schools of anarchism, anarcho-syndicalism is deeply rooted in revolutionary workers' action – syndicalism – by which workers seek to gain control of the economy. The basic principles are solidarity, direct action and workers' self-management, and the main strategy is the general strike. Its ultimate aim is to abolish the wage system, which anarcho-syndicalists regard as wage slavery. Originating in the writings of Proudhon, anarcho-syndicalism appeared in Spain as the Confederación Nacional del Trabajo (CNT), later merging with the International Workers' Association (IWA), and informing the Industrial Workers of the World (IWW) in the USA. During the 1920s, mass anarchist unions were created across Latin America and syndicalist-led strikes took place in Germany, Portugal, Spain, Italy and France. The rise of fascism in Europe saw anarcho-syndicalism driven underground almost everywhere except in Spain, where the CNT played a leading role in the Spanish Revolution and Civil War. Today Noam Chomsky is probably the best-known anarcho-syndicalist.

The black cat emblem of the IWW.

Collectivist anarchism

Pierre-Joseph Proudhon famously stated that 'property is theft', which remains a popular anarchist belief today. The issue of ownership is a key concern of anarchist theory. Collectivist anarchism, or anarcho-collectivism, advocates the abolition of the state, which will be overthrown through revolution, following which all property would be seized, including the means of production. In place of private ownership and control, collectivist anarchists advocate the collective ownership, management and control of the means of production by workers, through workers' collectives.

Workers would receive salaries based on the amount of time they contribute to production, following the maxim 'to everyone according to their labour'. Salaries would be used to buy goods in a communal market. Collectivist anarchism is mainly associated with Russian anarchist Mikhail Bakunin, who argued that religion, capitalism and the state are oppressive institutions that must be smashed if people are to be free.

All property is theft

Anarcho-communism

Anarcho-communism, like most other strands of anarchism, is profoundly anti-capitalist and, as its name suggests, links to communism in its views of ownership. Promoted by Russian anarchists Peter Kropotkin (pictured) and Emma Goldman, it advocates abolition of the state, economic markets, money and capitalism in favour of common ownership of the means of production. Goldman, together with many other anarchists, also advocated the abolition of marriage. This strand of anarchism developed from radical socialist trends after the French Revolution but was first expressed during the First International, which brought together socialists, communists, anarchists and trade unionists. Anarcho-communists were influential during the 1936 Spanish Revolution, and were a major force in Aragon, Andulusia and Catalonia, with much of Spain's economy being placed under worker control. Worker committees ran factories, farming was collectivized and workers even ran hotels and restaurants. By 1939, however, anarcho-communism in Spain had been crushed.

Libertarianism and anarcho-capitalism

Despite being usually anti-capitalist, anarchism contains a substrand that favours capitalism, namely anarcho-capitalism. Its adherents consider the state to be an unnecessary evil that should be abolished, but favour a free-market economic system, including the principle of private property. American economist Murray Newton Rothbard was one of the main proponents of anarcho-capitalism. He combined individualist anarchism, classical liberalism and Austrian School economics to create a political and economic philosophy that stresses the importance of freedom from the state and coercive monopolies. More recently, anarcho-capitalism has been associated with the 'rolling-back-the-state' policies emerging from the neoliberalism of Ronald Reagan and Margaret Thatcher. Anarcho-capitalism is often linked to libertarianism, a political philosophy that views liberty as its primary political virtue. Libertarianism can be viewed as right-wing, reflecting an anti-state free-market position, or left-wing, reflecting calls for liberty and freedom.

Anarchist revolution

Anarchism is often associated with violent subversion – the image of a masked man with a smoking bomb remains a popular caricature. During the late 19th century a significant development occurred with the emergence of a doctrine known as 'propaganda of the deed', following the views of Italian anarchist Errico Malatesta. This led to a period of violent actions, beginning with rural insurrections intended to rouse the masses and leading to individual acts of terrorism.

Between the 1880s and 1914, individual anarchists assassinated several heads of state, including King Umberto I of Italy, French president Sadi Carnot, American president William McKinley, Spanish prime minister Antonio Canovas del Castillo, King Carlos I of Portugal and George I of Greece. By the late 1880s, key anarchists, including Peter Kropotkin, were distancing themselves from these acts. Emma Goldman (pictured) also revised her position, and by 1914 most anarchists had abandoned support for propaganda of the deed.

Totalitarianism

Authoritarianism and totalitarianism are distinct, but related, types of rule. Authoritarian politics is the exact reverse of the ideals of liberalism and libertarianism, in that it emphasizes the importance of authority and power above freedom, and the rule of law above personal decisions. What marks an authoritarian government or ruler as totalitarian, however, is when the state seeks total authority over society. Totalitarian regimes, such as dictators, military juntas and theocracies, place the authority of the state above the rights of the individual, using their power to dictate and control all aspects of people's public and private lives, including their attitudes, values and beliefs, and are intolerant of any opposition. All political ideologies, both left- and right-wing fall somewhere on the scale between authoritarianism and libertarianism, but few are genuinely totalitarian. Totalitarianism very often involves a strongly nationalistic or religious element, sometimes with very racist attitudes, and frequently leads to conflict with other nations.

Tyranny and police states

Although the term 'tyrant' originally had a neutral meaning in Ancient Greece, the behaviour of many absolute rulers rapidly gave it negative connotations. Tyrants were seen as ruling in their own interest, rather than that of their people, and often using oppressive force to maintain their authority and overcome opposition, so that today we describe such authoritarian methods as tyrannical. Totalitarian states are by definition authoritarian, and many are tyrannical in enforcing their rule, using police or military forces to the extent that they may be called 'police states'. Although definitions of what constitutes a police state are somewhat subjective, examples include Nazi Germany, the Soviet Union and its satellites, Augusto Pinochet's Chile, and North Korea. State control of every aspect of society in such totalitarian states requires a strict enforcement of draconian laws, including restrictions on mobility and communications, and severe penalties for law-breaking. This is administered by the police, and may also involve the use of the secret police and intelligence services.

Dictatorship

Within a totalitarian state, because individual rights and freedoms are restricted or even absent, the government wields considerable political power and is often concentrated to the authority of a small number of people, or even a single person, commonly referred to as a dictator. The majority of authoritarian regimes have charismatic leaders who have either spearheaded the regime's rise to power, seized the leadership or emerged from the ranks of the ruling elite. They are often seen as dictators although they may simply be the leaders or figureheads of an authoritarian government. It is not always the case that all totalitarian regimes have gained power by force: a number of dictators were initially elected and subsequently extended their powers. Also, although dictators and totalitarian governments are generally at the extreme left or right of the political spectrum, they may have moved to this position from a more moderate stance. They are characterized more by their authoritarian methods of governance than their actual socioeconomic policies.

Charlie Chaplin lampooned European fascist leaders in his 1940 film *The Great Dictator*.

One-party state

A distinguishing feature of all totalitarian governments is their intolerance of most forms of opposition. This is manifest in attitudes to free speech and freedom of the press and media, but most obvious in countries that have adopted some type of single-party system of government. This can be the effective quashing of opposition, while maintaining a facade of multiparty democracy, by a dominant party that controls and manipulates the electoral system or intimidates its opponents by force. Or it can be an outright one-party state, legitimized by its constitution, which outlaws all but the ruling party. Totalitarian regimes are generally strongly nationalistic, and the one-party state is most often justified on the grounds of national unity, or to represent the interest of the majority population. There are also ideological justifications, such as the Marxist belief that political parties other than the communist party represent the interests of capitalism and are inimical to the interests of the state, or the religious justification that a particular party or faction has a divine right to rule.

Fascism

Fascism emerged in Italy during the First World War at a time when Italian nationalists were seeking a comprehensive ideology to match their dream of a dynamic, modern state as the heir to Ancient Rome. Benito Mussolini, the charismatic founder and leader of the fascist movement, had been a prominent socialist, and rejected the materialism and injustice of liberal capitalism, but found communism incompatible with his extreme nationalist leanings. Instead, he proposed a corporatist economic system with employers and the workforce united in production for the nation, and a modernization of Italian industry as a foundation for the building of an Italian empire. In place of class struggle and party political conflict, he advocated 'Strength through Unity', as exemplified by the fasces, the bundle of twigs of the fascist emblem. The National Fascist Party seized power in Italy following the March to Rome in 1922, and Mussolini led the ultranationalist dictatorship until he was ousted in 1943. Fascism is now outlawed by the Italian constitution.

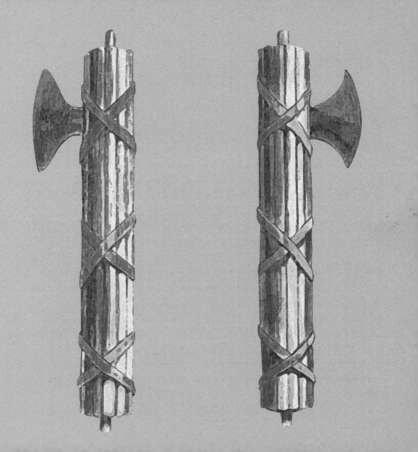

Nazism

Nazism also had its roots in the First World War and the nationalist politics of a charismatic leader, Adolf Hitler. Nazism developed quite separately from Italian fascism, evolving from the German Workers' Party, which later became the Nationalsozialistische Deutsche Arbeiterpartei (NSDAP), from which the word 'Nazi' is derived. Hitler shifted the NSDAP towards ultranationalism and a rejection of both communism and capitalism, which he denounced as Jewish conspiracies.

A year after a failed coup, he led the party to legitimate power in 1923, gaining support for the Nazi ideology of expansionist nationalism based on the idea of an Aryan 'master race'. Officially a revolutionary socialist movement, Nazism under Hitler became increasingly overtly right-wing and authoritarian, and the nationalism more racist. Today Nazism is synonymous with extreme right-wing authoritarianism, coupled with extreme ethnic nationalism, characterized by notions of racial supremacy and antisemitism.

Communist totalitarianism

In Marxist theory, socialism is seen as a transitional stage between capitalism and the establishment of true communism. Sometimes described as 'the dictatorship of the proletariat', this stage was interpreted by some as implying a totalitarian rule to consolidate the system against opposition. In Soviet Russia, Joseph Stalin used state violence to intimidate and eradicate opposition, installing himself as the dictatorial leader of a totalitarian communist state. Similarly, Mao Zedong (pictured) implemented Marxist/Leninist policies with a greater degree of nationalism to establish a Chinese totalitarian state, and Fidel Castro established a one-party socialist state in Cuba. North Korea is arguably one of the most repressive of all communist totalitarian states. On gaining independence from the Soviet Union in 1948, the Democratic People's Republic of Korea was modelled on Stalin's authoritarian communism. The dictatorship is now dynastic, with the title of Supreme Leader passing from Kim Il-sung to his son Kim Jong-il and then his grandson Kim Jong-un.

Religious totalitarianism

Before the Enlightenment, and with the exception of the democracies of the Ancient Greeks and Romans, almost every absolute ruler could be described as more or less totalitarian. Many used religious 'divine right' as justification for their authority, which in Europe meant power was under the control of the Catholic church.

Nowadays, however, this kind of religious totalitarianism is restricted to Islam, and the very few authoritarian Islamic states enforcing a strict adherence to sharia. These include Arabic nations, such as Saudi Arabia and Qatar, and Sudan, Afghanistan when under the control of the Taliban, and debatably Iran. What characterizes these regimes as totalitarian is the absence of democratic processes, such as political parties, and the rigorous control over people's private as well as public life, but especially the outlawing of apostasy – turning away from the faith – which can be interpreted as outlawing all infidels and so criminalizing opposition.

IOANNES XXI· DICTVS XXII· PONT· CXCVIII·
ANNO DOMINI MCCCXVI·

Coup d'état

While some totalitarian regimes have been democratically elected and become gradually more authoritarian, others have seized power after a revolution or civil war has overthrown the previous government or ruler. Some have seized power from within, in a coup d'état. Unlike a revolution, which is characterized by a 'bottom-up' popular movement to remove an existing power, a coup, sometimes also known as a putsch, is when a faction within the establishment illegally seizes power and forces a 'top-down' change of regime, imposed by a minority of insiders on the majority population.

In order to retain power, the usurpers almost invariably introduce authoritarian laws and take forcible measures to prevent resistance. As with most totalitarian regimes, they are usually led by a charismatic figure such as Napoleon (opposite), who assumes the role of dictator, or even emperor, and more often than not as commander-in-chief of the armed forces, to intimidate any potential opposition.

Military juntas

It is always wise to have military backing to enforce unpopular authoritarian control and many dictators have courted the armed forces both before and during their rule. Some, such as Idi Amin Dada and Francisco Franco, had a military background themselves, which they stressed by being frequently seen in uniform, and even civilian dictators have accorded themselves a spurious military rank. But the military themselves do sometimes come to power in a coup d'état, particularly if they have lost confidence in their civilian rulers. The military leaders then form a government known as a junta, taking over control of the state, as happened under the colonels in Greece between 1967–74 and Chile in 1973–90. A military junta is by nature authoritarian and hierarchical, and once in power difficult to remove. Juntas often come to power at times of national crisis or conflict, such as during a civil war, justifying their takeover as politically neutral and acting in the national interest, but this may be a pretext for an ambitious faction within the forces to seize dictatorial power.

Nation, race and religion

Humans are social animals. We tend to form social groups that range from small families with a shared inheritance, to organizations with shared beliefs, interests or aims, and entire nations with a shared history or culture. We all, to some extent, tend to identify ourselves by our membership of these groups. And the nations, regions, towns and villages we live in are defined not simply by their borders on a map, but the attachments and allegiances of the people within them.

Our attachment to a particular group is often a source of pride, and a willingness to defend it from criticism or attack can be an important factor in social cohesion, enabling people to live together as a society. It is inevitable, then, that the way that we organize and govern these societies – our political systems – is influenced by those things that have brought them together in the first place, and which make them distinct from other societies.

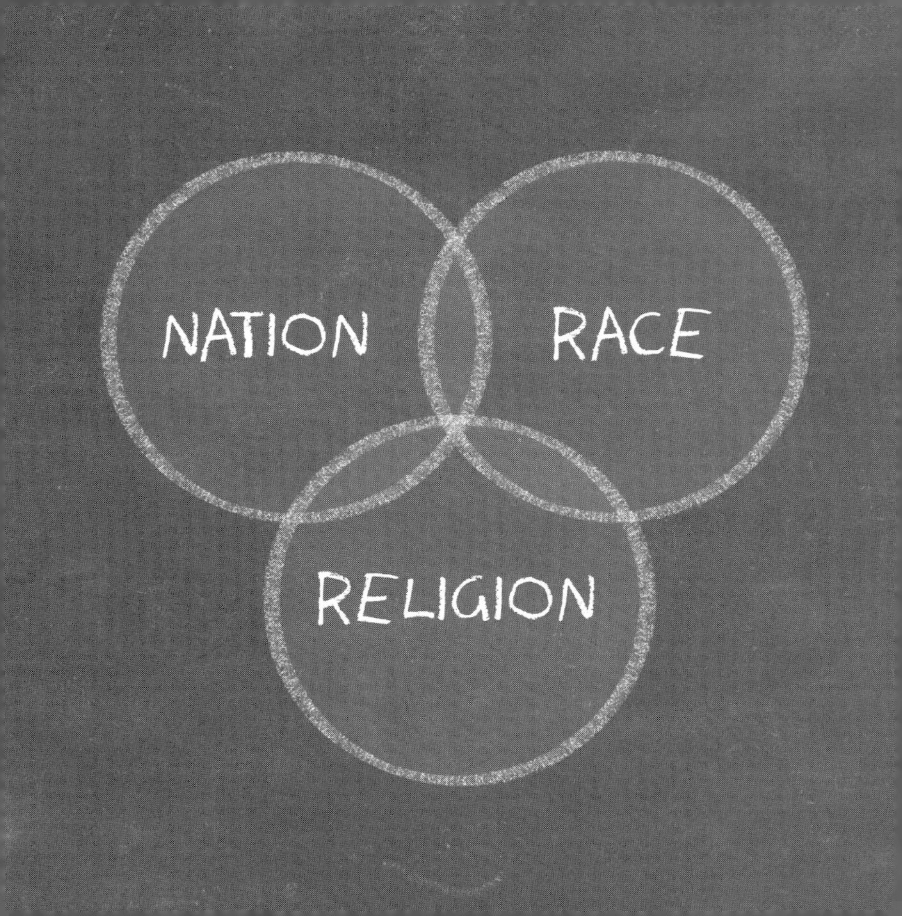
NATION
RACE
RELIGION

Nationalism

Today, we tend to think of the nation states as the political units that make up the world, and people tend to consider their nation as a significant factor in how they identify themselves. This attachment to national identity can become the basis for a political ideology – nationalism – with nationalist movements and parties aiming to strengthen or protect a sense of national unity. Many nationalist movements have arisen as a reaction against oppression, particularly in the fight for liberation from an imperial power, or to establish the independence of a distinct minority group within a larger nation. Others have their roots in conflict with neighbouring countries, or to gather support for expansionism. While nationalism can be a positive force for social cohesion and against oppression, it also has the potential to become xenophobic. In many European countries, the perceived threat of immigration and multiculturalism to so-called indigenous populations has given rise to more or less racist nationalist parties, often with far-right authoritarian leanings.

Patriotism

Nationalism can be seen as the political manifestation of feelings of national identity, a specific ideology on which various political movements and parties are founded. Patriotism, while closely linked to the concept of nationalism, is different in that it is not a particular belief, but the way in which people show their attachment to their nation. In a sense, nationalism is built on the idea that a nation is there for the benefit of its people, whereas patriotism is the idea that the people are there for the nation.

Indeed, nationalism can call on patriotism for support, which can be so deeply ingrained that it becomes 'my country, right or wrong'. Like nationalism, patriotism involves an element of pride, but also carries notions of loyalty and even devotion to the nation, and its institutions and symbols of state. Many nations have a formal oath or pledge of allegiance, which aspiring citizens are required to take confirming their duty to protect and defend their country.

Ethnic nationalism

Nationalism is not defined by national borders and can take a variety of forms. Any social group is defined by the thing or things its members have in common, and national identity is strongly linked to the idea of common characteristics. Ethnic nationalism is a form of nationalism that defines the nation in terms of a shared heritage, both as a common ancestry and a common culture, which together are often known as ethnicity.

Ethnic identity has a long history, defining the differences between tribal groups from which our nations have evolved, and on very basic level are based on kinship or 'blood relationships'. Consequently, there is often a racial element in any form of ethnic nationalism. Allied to this, however, is the notion of heritage: the culture, customs, religion and language of a society. And because ethnicity has evolved organically over a long period, it is deeply rooted in societies, transcending national borders, and so is sometimes at odds with political ideas of nationality.

Civic nationalism

Nationalism based on notions of ethnicity can lead to xenophobic attitudes and foster conflict between different ethnic groups. A shared cultural and racial heritage can also be exclusive and intolerant of 'outsiders'. Liberal political thinkers propose instead a more inclusive form of civic nationalism. In line with the Enlightenment tradition of rationalism, they define a community as comprising all who live in it regardless of their ethnicity. Thus, national identity is not created by accident of birth but is decided upon voluntarily, by moving to or choosing to remain in a country, or civic nation.

Civic nationalism began to gain ground in the 19th century, as an alternative to ethnic nationalism, especially in countries such as the USA, as the young nation asserted its independence with a distinct identity, a strong liberal tradition and an ethnically diverse population. In more recent times, there have been calls for a greater emphasis on civic nationalism to counter the rise of extreme ethnic nationalist movements.

Expansionist nationalism

Nationalist movements frequently arise as resistance to imperial or colonial occupation of what the inhabitants consider to be sovereign territory. Nationalism may, however, also be part of the ideology of an occupying power. Aggressive nationalism is often a component of expansionist policies, playing on feelings of patriotism and superiority. In contrast to liberal nationalism, expansionist nationalism tends to be overtly chauvinistic, and a pretext for acquiring territory or gaining dominance over other nations.

Implied, and sometimes explicitly stated, is a notion that some nations are superior to others and have a right to exert power over them or encroach upon their territory. This was most noticeable in the empire-building of the 19th century, when it was a matter of pride for European nations to expand their influence by acquiring colonies around the world. Nationalism, both civic and ethnic, also figured in the Japanese and German military expansionism that led to the Second World War.

Imperialism and colonialism

Some nations assert their superiority over others, by extending their borders and invading their neighbours to build empires. This urge for imperialism is driven by a desire for not only ideological dominance, but also economic gain, through acquisition of resources and territory. And with advances in transportation, empires have been built not simply by expanding into neighbouring countries, but also by colonizing more distant ones. Spain and Portugal, for example, colonized South America, while other European powers acquired territories in North America and Asia, and later with the 'Scramble for Africa', global empires were formed. This kind of colonialism established networks of international trade that survived the empires themselves. Even after independence, colonies maintained trading and cultural links with their former masters, and with one another, sometimes formally as in the formation of the British Commonwealth. The influence of colonialism was also reflected in the political and cultural institutions of the newly independent nations.

The 1948 voyage of the *Empire Windrush* began a wave of migration into post-War Britain from across its dwindling Empire.

Slavery

The history of slavery is as long as that of empires. It was common in all the civilizations of the ancient world, providing a cheap labour force generally consisting of people taken from a conquered nation. With the advent of the great trading empires in the 15th century, however, the nature of slavery changed fundamentally, as slaves became increasingly considered as a commodity that could be traded. This grew in importance as European empires colonized new countries and required a large labour force to supplement local workers.

The slave trade became big business, with fortunes being made by European slavers moving staggeringly large numbers of African slaves across the Atlantic to work in the cotton fields and sugar plantations of North America. The move to abolish the slave trade helped to shape liberal politics in the 19th century, but the change slavery made to the demographic of especially America and the Caribbean profoundly influenced political attitudes to race and ethnicity to the present day.

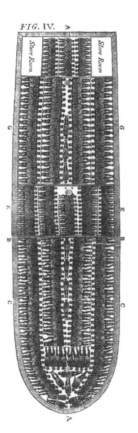

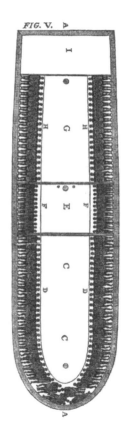

Anti-colonial and post-colonial nationalism

In their struggle for independence from the empires of the old European powers, many countries experienced a surge in nationalism – an assertion of their specific national identities. Interestingly, in the USA – the first nation to successfully break from colonial rule – it was the settlers rather than the indigenous population who led the revolt. These were mainly European emigrants, inspired by Enlightenment ideas of rights and freedom, so the nationalism they inspired was civic rather than ethnic.

Elsewhere inspired by the American revolt, the nationalist movements in South America and the Caribbean, and later in Africa, followed ethnic lines, which are still reflected in the nationalist politics of those countries today. Nationalist movements also emerged in Europe in the 19th century as countries sought to break from the Ottoman and Russian empires, and more recently as eastern European countries asserted their independence from the Soviet bloc.

Independence and self-determination

As more and more countries won independence from the old empires, they asserted their new-found freedom by establishing new nation states on their own terms – not just installing a new local leader or government, but setting up a system of government from scratch. The precedent for this right to self-determination was set by the US Declaration of Independence, closely followed by its Constitution. But this right was by no means universally recognized. In 1823, the USA issued the Monroe Doctrine, stating that any colonization or interference in its affairs (or in those of other new nations in the Americas) by European countries would be regarded as an act of aggression, effectively proclaiming its status as a sovereign state. The old imperial powers, however, hung on to their empires elsewhere and maintained influence even in some ex-colonies. Pressure for international recognition to the right of self-determination increased through the 20th century, supported by the USA and Britain, and was finally enshrined in international law after the foundation of the United Nations.

British Prime Minister Harold McMillan acknowledged the need for self-determination in his 'Winds of Change' speech, made during a 1960 trip to Africa.

Race and politics

What are now loosely referred to as 'racial' issues became more important politically through the effects of imperialism and the slave trade, and the nationalist movements prompted by them. The term 'race' is itself controversial and has been used to refer to many different aspects of what would be more accurately called ethnicity – involving culture, language and religion, as well as physical differences between different groups, such as skin colour.

The attitude that one ethnic group is superior to another forms a dark side of ethnic nationalism, and can be reflected in the relations between countries of predominantly different ethnicities. Even within countries, minority ethnic groups are often treated with suspicion or hostility. This may result in overt – and sometimes state-sanctioned – discrimination and segregation, denying certain people the same rights and freedoms as the majority. Less obvious forms of prejudice put race and ethnicity squarely on the political agenda.

Civil rights movement

Despite its avowed commitment to equality and rights set out in its Declaration of Independence, the USA denied rights to all but privileged white men until well into the 20th century. While it took a civil war to achieve the abolition of slavery, the substantial black population remained without equal rights and suffered segregation in the southern states from the notorious 'Jim Crow laws'.

At the beginning of the 20th century, black activists such as W.E.B. Du Bois helped to instigate campaigns for equal rights, which gained momentum to become a major civil rights movement. Under the leadership of Martin Luther King in the 1960s, segregation was brought to an end. Similar struggles for civil rights were ongoing, notably in South Africa, where the white-minority government's oppressive system of apartheid was finally brought to an end by pressure from an international anti-apartheid movement and the inspiration of the leader of the African National Congress party, Nelson Mandela.

Ethnic discrimination

By the end of the 20th century, many of the goals of the civil rights movement (see page 290) appeared to have been achieved, in theory at least. The majority of democratic countries had adopted legislation that granted equal rights to all people regardless of ethnicity, generally alongside laws against discrimination on the grounds of ethnicity. But there is still some way to go before civil rights are universally and comprehensively protected. Attitudes are slowly changing, but public and even official observance is lagging behind the law. Even in countries that are officially opposed to ethnic discrimination, old prejudices and suspicions remain entrenched in their institutions, with the effect that the law is not always strictly or fairly enforced. Minority groups are more likely to be stopped and searched, or convicted of crimes, and less likely to have access to the best universities or the best jobs. Immigration laws are often seen as targeted at minority ethnic groups, as are those banning conspicuous or 'provocative' signs of religion, such as the *hijab*, or headscarf.

Positive discrimination

Despite the widespread adoption of anti-discrimination legislation, minority ethnic groups (and women) are still in practice at a disadvantage in many areas of life. This is particularly noticeable in employment, where the top posts are occupied almost exclusively by members of the predominant (usually white-European) ethnic group, and minorities are more than statistically likely to be in lower-paid or unpleasant jobs. Legislation is clearly not effective in preventing discrimination, so to try to rectify the inequality, some countries have used a system of positive discrimination. India, which has a very ethnically diverse population, operates a system of quotas of educational places and jobs for the various ethnic groups; elsewhere applicants for vacancies from minority ethnic groups are given preferential treatment. Although these 'affirmative action' schemes have been successful in ironing out inequalities, they have also been accused of unfairly tipping the balance, and run the risk of increasing rather than decreasing prejudice against minority ethnic groups.

Multiculturalism

One of the hopes of nations that were founded on a notion of civic rather than ethnic national identity is that it would promote inclusiveness, and minimize discrimination against ethnic minorities. Implicit in this idea, for many states, was a notion of homogeneity or uniformity, with the nation as a 'melting pot' in which different ethnic groups would blend together. But what emerged in many nations with diverse ethnic populations was a multicultural society, in which people retained their ethnic identity (customs, religion and language) within the wider civic nationality.

Multiculturalism can minimize ethnic discrimination and xenophobia, when the diversity of ethnic groups is recognized as a complement to civic nationalism. Acknowledging the right to observe different cultural customs can increase tensions, particularly if institutions, such as faith schools, separate groups from the wider community, and minority and especially immigrant groups can become 'ghettoized'.

Migration

Since the 19th century, improvements in transport have meant that huge numbers of migrants have left their home countries to seek a better life. Young nations such as the USA and Australia have become prosperous through their acceptance of immigrants, and older countries in Europe have at one time or another been reliant on an immigrant workforce. But in recent times, many countries have imposed severe restrictions on immigration, which is increasingly seen as a problem rather than a boon. Instead of importing labour, it has become more economical to outsource production to another country, freeing up more of the domestic workforce to staff the service industries. Immigrants have consequently been regarded as a threat to local jobs for local people, and a drain on resources. A distinction is sometimes made between these 'economic migrants' and refugees from natural disasters, or asylum seekers fleeing oppression. This has become a major issue for some right-wing nationalist political parties, who point to social problems arising from multiculturalism.

Zionism

While in the USA and Africa the driving force behind the civil rights movements was one of white-European supremacy over black-Africans, elsewhere there were other racial tensions. Jewish people had suffered discrimination, long before even African colonization. Displaced Jewish communities in Europe and parts of Asia had been frequently persecuted, segregated and even confined to ghettoes – discrimination so widespread that it has its own name: antisemitism. Some Jews campaigned for the establishment of a separate homeland. Zionism, the movement pressing for a Jewish state of Israel, gained political support from certain quarters, but was vigorously opposed by others, including many Jews. The argument centred on the question of Jewish identity: is it defined by race, religion or culture, and is it a nationality? In the wake of the Nazi Holocaust, the state of Israel was founded in 1948, and continues to support its existence and security in the face of criticism and actual violence directed against it, which some believe are antisemitic.

The role of religion

Perhaps more than any other aspect of ethnic identity, religion has the ability to be a positive force for social cohesion and, at the same time, very socially divisive. Religion is traditionally a central part of many societies, and the shared faith underlying their social and political structures not only unites communities, but also improves relations across national boundaries. But differences of religious belief, even on minor points of doctrine, arouse strong passions and can lead to persecution of religious minorities, xenophobia and conflict.

It is no coincidence that many of the internal tensions within countries are between communities divided along religious lines, nor that international conflicts are similarly over religious as much as political boundaries. For these reasons, a large number of liberal democracies have taken an official line that religion and politics are best kept separate, in so far as that is possible. However, a significant number of states around the world still recognize a role for religion in their political systems.

The laws of God and the laws of Man

One of the roles of religion in society is to provide a moral code and a set of rules for behaviour, such as the Ten Commandments. These, for believers, are the laws that God has revealed to us and, as such, have divine authority. In contrast, the laws decided by governments are man-made and, for the believer, lack the same authority. Reconciling conflicting earthly and divine laws became more of a problem as societies developed political systems separate from their religions.

This was particularly true in the medieval Christian world, where the Catholic church was intricately involved in political power. Christian philosophers suggested that man-made laws do have authority over earthly affairs, but that divine laws presented the overarching spiritual code; man's law is a part of God's creation, and so supplements, rather than contradicts God's immutable law. This solution gave governments some authority, while the Church – as the moral arbiter that shaped its laws – was not excluded from political affairs.

The divine right to rule

In almost every culture, it has been believed at some time that a leader is given authority by God to rule over his or her people. In Ancient China, this was described as the 'mandate of heaven', which was bestowed upon a just emperor – if his rule was unjust this was withdrawn and his legitimacy removed. Because of this widely held belief in a divine right of kings, the authority of absolute monarchs, given by God, trumps the authority of political leaders, whose authority is merely earthly.

This gave considerable power to monarchs – and the Pope, who not only has divine authority, but is also considered infallible – placing them effectively above the law. From the late medieval period, in Europe at least, that power was challenged. Only a handful of absolute monarchs supported by the claim of a divine right to rule remain in power today. There are still many royal families whose privileged position is justified by 'the grace of God', and a lingering tradition even in some democracies that political leaders should have some form of divine approval.

State religion

The connection between politics and religion runs very deep. Religions have provided societies with the moral code that underpins their laws. In many cases, there is a predominant religion in a country that is intrinsic to its national identity and cultural heritage, even if it is now only practised by a minority of the population. The United Kingdom, for example, is often considered a 'Christian country' despite its multicultural make-up.

Some faiths are endorsed as official, state religions, in a similar way to the adoption of a language as the official language. This may be a formal acknowledgement that gives little or no real status to the religion or its clerics, where the religion plays a purely ceremonial role, or where representatives of the faith may play some part in the secular government. Today, most countries with a state religion are Islamic, but there are some countries, notably the UK, which have retained an established Christian church.

Rowan Williams,
Archbishop of Canterbury
between 2002 and 2012,
at the UK State Opening
Of Parliament.

Secular states

As republics replaced the old monarchies, the political power of religions, and particularly the Christian church, was increasingly seen as incompatible with the idea of democracy. Many of these new nations followed the lead of the USA in establishing themselves as secular states, excluding religion from the political process while adopting a strict neutrality on matters of faith. This follows the liberal principle of giving all citizens an equal right to practise their chosen religion, or none, without favour or discrimination. The majority of modern liberal democracies are either founded on or have adopted the idea of a secular state. However, some have gone further in the separation of state from religion, declaring themselves officially atheist. The Soviet Union, China and North Korea have all adopted this form of secularism, and tolerated religion to a greater or lesser extent, while Albania actually banned religion in 1945. But religion continues to have an influence, even in the most secular of states: in 1954, the USA amended its pledge of allegiance to include the phrase 'one nation under God'.

Theocracy

Literally meaning 'rule by God', theocracy is the form of government in which the clergy of a particular religion rule over the civil state. More than simply a recognition of an official state religion, it is an adoption of that religion as the source of the official policy of the state, administered by its leaders. The officials of a theocratic government are believed to be divinely chosen and guided, and their authority, like the divine right of kings, is God-given rather than granted by the people. The laws that they make and enforce are laid down by their faith, and support its doctrine.

Christian theocracy was once the distinguishing feature of medieval Europe, but is now confined to the Vatican state. Today, the idea is more associated with Islam – regimes, such as the Taliban in Afghanistan or the Ayatollahs in Iran, where clerics are accorded considerable political power. Although absolute theocracy is rare, even in Islamic states, clerics continue to have significant influence in many countries.

Islam and sharia law

The civic laws of most countries in the world today have been decided by people – governments, legislators, judges and constitution writers – rather than set by God or dictated by the doctrine of a religion. Nevertheless, these civic laws often bear a resemblance to the moral code of the predominant faith or faiths of that country; furthermore, some laws, such as those against murder, theft and so on, are universal. In Islamic states, the religious law of Islam – sharia – is the primary source of legislation. Taken from the Qur'an and the teachings of the Prophet Muhammad in the Sunnah, sharia is accepted in these countries as the infallible word of God, which requires no human additions and cannot be contradicted. Many devout Muslims believe that sharia must be observed over and above the civic law. Unlike other religious laws, it is more than simply a code of ethics and personal morality; it includes rules for political and economic conduct. Sharia constitutes a large part of the legislation of several Arabic countries, and is the basis for laws in most Islamic countries.

Religious fundamentalism

The liberal notion of allowing freedom of religion has helped to soften attitudes towards the separation of religion and state, and to a large extent religions have gradually accepted ideas – such as attitudes to sexuality and gender equality – that previously were unthinkable. But there are factions within some religions that do not accept these changes, and believe that the doctrine of their faith is immutable.

At the beginning of the 20th century, the term 'fundamentalism' first appeared to refer to some of the Christian communities in the USA who insisted on a literal interpretation of Christian scriptures. More recently, the word has been more associated with Islam, and a particularly hardline observance of the Qur'an and sharia. It has also been used to describe some of the more extremely orthodox branches of Judaism. Because their beliefs often clash with the values of modern democracy – and those of other religions – religious fundamentalist movements have become a significant political force.

Anti-modernism

One of the distinguishing features of nearly every religious fundamentalist movement is a desire to turn the clock back. Fundamentalism is most prevalent in the Abrahamic religions – Judaism, Christianity and Islam – which had been established centuries before the advent of modern political systems. It is the same Enlightenment ideas that challenge these faiths the most, and to some extent force change upon them.

Modernism, for these fundamentalists, takes the form of liberal attitudes to rights and freedom at the expense of morality and traditional values. Some, such as the Amish and Mennonite communities in the USA, have simply cut themselves off from the modern world they disagree with. Others, however, are more aggressive in their opposition to modernity, calling for the repeal of what they see as immoral secular liberalism, and even democracy itself, and a return to the values and ethics on which their religion is founded.

The Christian right

Conservative Christianity, including traditionalists within the Catholic church and some Nonconformist Protestant groups, exists throughout the Christian world, but largely limits itself to theological rather than political disputes. In the USA, however, a fundamentalist movement among American Protestants gained considerable support – as well as rejecting liberal theology, it took a stance against what it saw as a decline in moral and cultural standards in society caused by liberal politics. The popularity of these largely evangelical groups gained momentum and, helped by the media exposure of 'televangelists' from the 1970s, built up considerable financial resources and political influence. Movements such as the American Christian Cause, Christian Voice and the Moral Majority formed what was dubbed the new Christian Right, which increasingly involved itself in political activism. As well as campaigning for changes to laws that are antithetical to its beliefs, it has actively supported conservative Republican candidates in elections, in return for influence over policy.

Islamic fundamentalism

An extremely conservative approach to Islamic teaching led to the formation of the Wahhabi movement as early as the 18th century, and it has since gained a large following worldwide. Its fundamentalist ideology is behind theocratic Islamic states, such as Saudi Arabia and Qatar, and has been widely adopted in other countries, including Pakistan.

However, the term 'Islamic fundamentalism' has today taken on a different meaning, referring to revolutionary and often violent Islamist movements – more accurately called 'radical Islam'. As a fundamentalist movement forcibly opposing the influence of Western liberal modernity, radical Islam first gained prominence with the revolution in Iran in 1979, which ousted the Shah and replaced him with a theocratic government of Ayatollahs. Since then, numerous movements, both Sunni and Shia, have fought for the formation of Islamic states, including terrorist networks, such as Al Qaeda, Boko Haram and the Islamic State of Iraq and the Levant (IS, or ISIS or ISIL).

Jihadism and terrorism

The concept of *jihad* in Islam, in simple terms, is the religious duty of all Muslims to struggle and resist in order to protect the faith from harm. In the latter part of the 20th century, this was taken by radical Islam as a call to arms, especially after the establishment of the state of Israel and the spread of Western-style democracy into Islamic countries.

Outright conflict was, until the 21st century, confined largely to the Middle Eastern countries, but terrorism increasingly became a threat elsewhere. A turning point was the September 11 attacks on the World Trade Center in New York City in 2001, coordinated by the Al Qaeda network. This marked the beginning of a global 'War on Terror' declared by President George W. Bush, which in turn was met with further terrorist attacks on Western targets, and the recruitment of Islamic 'jihadists', not only from Islamic countries but also from those 'radicalized' by influential fundamentalist preachers in the West.

Gender politics

Women make up more than half the world's population and yet for most of human history, they have been regarded and treated as 'second-class citizens', and denied legal, social and economic rights, and access to the political process. They were denied these rights purely and simply because they were women – the justification, seemingly, that women were an inferior and weaker sex, incapable of competing with men in the harsh world of politics. Women's struggle to overcome this situation gave rise to a new type of politics – one that is based primarily on sex and gender rather than, for example, class or race. Often seen as synonymous, sex and gender are quite different. While sex refers to biological maleness or femaleness, gender refers to socially or culturally imposed roles. This distinction has given rise to gender politics – a politics that challenges gender roles as a means of subordinating not only women, but also gays, lesbians, transsexuals and others who are discriminated against purely because of their sexuality or gender assumptions.

Patriarchy

Literally meaning 'rule of the father', patriarchy refers to the universal political structure, which privileges men at the expense of women. It was originally coined by anthropologists to describe a particular social structure in which one man, the father, holds power over the family. Many feminists argue, however, that all societies are patriarchal because within those society's institutions, men have control over women's lives.

In her 1970 book *Sexual Politics*, Kate Millett analysed 'patriarchy as a political institution' – 'politics', here, referring to all power-structured relationships and therefore leading to a 'relationship of dominance and subordination' between the sexes. Clearly there are some societies where women have greater privileges, rights and powers than others but many feminists argue that, within a patriarchy, it is only a token power and not embedded in the dominant ideology. Such feminists believe that women cannot be fully independent until the patriarchy is ended.

Feminism

As a political movement feminism is based on the belief that the relationship between the sexes is one of inequality, with men dominating women. Feminism seeks to challenge and change this situation and bring an end to sexism, discrimination and injustices against women in all areas of society, from political institutions through to work, education and the family. Feminism contains different strands, reflecting differences of opinion over the causes of women's oppression and how to overcome it. 'Equal rights' feminism is the oldest tradition, which seeks to obtain the same political, legal and economic rights as men; Marxist/socialist feminism sees class as well as gender as a source of women's oppression; while Radical feminism seeks to redefine politics and abolish the patriarchy. Sometimes criticized for being white, middle-class and heterosexual, feminism has developed black women's groups and LGBT feminist strands. Feminism's impact on politics has been enormous, from achieving the vote to equal pay legislation and opposing female genital mutilation.

The rights of women

During the 18th century a new political philosophy, liberalism, emerged promoting the idea of human rights. It found its greatest expression in the French Revolution with the Declaration of the Rights of Man and of the Citizen. Promoted by Tom Paine in his influential book *Rights of Man* (1791), this philosophy completely failed to include the rights of women, however, who at this time had no political or legal rights at all.

French revolutionary Olympe de Gouges had issued a Declaration of the Rights of Women in 1791 in an attempt to force the revolutionary Assembly to include women in its calls for citizens' rights, but it failed. So it fell to Englishwoman Mary Wollstonecraft (pictured) to put women's rights on the political agenda for the first time. Countering Paine, in 1792 she published *A Vindication of the Rights of Woman* in which she protested the 'domestic tyranny' that kept women dependent on men, and called for them to have equal rights in work, education and politics.

The fight for the vote

By the 1860s, increasing numbers of women in Britain and America were channelling their energies into the fight for the vote and the right to stand for electoral office. It was a long hard battle that met with considerable opposition and even brutality from the public, press and police. In Britain, thousands of women organized within Millicent Fawcett's National Union of Suffrage Societies (NUWSS). Known as 'suffragists', they relied on peaceful law-abiding tactics, such as petitioning and lobbying sympathetic MPs. Others organized within the smaller Women's Social and Political Union (WSPU) of Emmeline and Christabel Pankhurst. The WSPU chose militant tactics. Members, nicknamed 'suffragettes', heckled MPs, rushed the House of Commons, demonstrated and went to prison in their hundreds, where many were forcibly fed after going on hunger strike. The years of struggle finally paid off. In 1918, British women over 30 gained the vote, though it was not until 1928 that they had the vote on equal terms with men. American women gained the vote in 1920.

Equality and difference

The idea of equality is a fundamental value of liberal politics and much of women's political activity has been directed towards achieving full equality with men. However, the concept of equality has been problematic. Feminists have pointed to the fact that there are also differences between women in class, race and sexuality. Equal rights within the law therefore become meaningless without ensuring equal opportunities.

Many feminists argue that biological differences should not be taken into account, for fear of making women into a 'special case' and hence marginalizing them. While some feminists welcomed, for example, the appointment of a Minister for Women, others saw it as patronizing. However, it is also argued that in today's world there are social, economic and cultural reasons why some issues can be seen as primarily affecting women, among them rape, domestic violence, pornography and female genital mutilation (FGM) and that these must be recognized and addressed.

An unequal world

On a global level, according to United Nations statistics, women do two-thirds of the world's work, yet receive only 10 per cent of the income, and own only 1 per cent of the means of production. Women also make up approximately two-thirds of the 1.4 million people worldwide living in extreme poverty. After nearly 200 years of women's political movements there are still glaring instances of inequality between the sexes.

In the UK, in 2015, more than 40 years after the Equal Pay Act of 1970, the gap between men and women's earnings stood at 19.1 per cent. American women earned around 80 per cent of their male counterparts. Despite challenges to gender stereotyping, women still do most of the unpaid work in the home, and when they return to employment are most likely to work in lower-paid, often part-time, jobs. The glass ceiling is very much in evidence with only a small percentage achieving top jobs. Research indicates that most women cite gender stereotyping as the major hurdle.

 % population

% wages

Women in power

In 1979, more than 60 years since women first gained the vote, Margaret Thatcher became Britain's first woman prime minister. However, since antiquity a number of strong-minded women have held powerful positions, either because of birth – Hatshepsut, Queen Elizabeth 1 and Queen Victoria – or as a result of fighting through male-dominated political structures – Golda Meir, Indira Gandhi, Aung San Suu Kyi and Benazir Bhutto (opposite). Yet these women are exceptions; by and large women remain under-represented in all governments.

In 2015, only 20 per cent of parliamentarians and 15 heads of government were women, and only 20 per cent of local government officials were female. In the UK, only one in five MPs are women, and there have been strenuous attempts to encourage more women into politics. Evidence indicates that female politicians face sexual harassment and discrimination on a daily basis, and unless these practices and the institutions themselves are reformed, women will be slow to take part.

Second- and third-wave feminism

The history of feminism is often described as a series of waves. The first wave covered the period 1850–1920 with campaigns for legal and political rights, including the vote. Initially known as the Women's Liberation Movement, the second wave emerged in the 1960s, influenced by books such as Simone de Beauvoir's *The Second Sex* and Betty Friedan's *The Feminine Mystique*. Second-wave feminists, organizing around a view that the personal is political, broadened political concerns to reflect women's lived experiences. They sought to liberate women from conventional and discriminatory roles within marriage, the family and work, and put issues such as reproductive rights and control over their own bodies onto the political agenda. Campaigns focused on healthcare, abortion, rape, domestic violence, pornography and abuse. In the 1980s there was a backlash against feminism, but from the 1990s a new, so-called third wave emerged. Including young women and women of colour, third-wave feminists have radically challenged heterosexuality and conventional gender roles.

Sex and gender

By definition, feminism and gender politics have put sex and gender under the microscope to explore and challenge received notions about masculinity and femininity. While sex refers to biological, anatomical differences, gender is a social construct that describes and defines the emotional and psychological expectations of a given culture towards physical maleness or femaleness. This may be as simple as a widespread assumption that women are 'naturally' emotional, peaceful, caring and passive, while men are less emotional, independent, active and aggressive. Feminists argue that, based on these kinds of assumptions, patriarchal societies impose gender appropriate roles on women and men in all areas of life, from family roles through to schooling, work, sexuality and political activity – an imposition that has discriminated against women and trapped men, too. Feminist activists have fought traditional sexual roles, particularly heterosexuality and gender stereotyping, as a means of liberating women and enabling some men to challenge socially imposed roles as well.

Sexuality and politics

Sexuality is a profoundly political issue because it is used as a basis for discrimination. The gay rights movement emerged in the late 1960s, advocating equal rights for gay men, lesbians, bisexuals and transgender persons. In 1969, a defining moment occurred when police raided the Stonewall Inn, a gay bar in New York. Nearly 400 people resisted over several nights, and the American gay rights movement was born. It subsequently spread worldwide. Gay rights activists have campaigned on many issues: anti-gay legislation, discriminatory practices in employment, housing and other aspects of civil society, bans on military service for gays, the lowering of the age of consent and same-sex civil partnerships and marriages. Since the 1980s, attitudes have changed and in the USA, Canada, Britain, Iceland and Belgium, openly gay individuals have held high political office. Since 1989, starting with Norway, many countries have legalized civil partnerships and same-sex marriages, most recently in Ireland in 2015. Virulent anti-gay laws, however, still exist in Russia, Iran and Uganda.

Ecology

Ecology is the scientific study of how organisms and their environment interact. Over the last 50 or so years, increasing concern about human impact on the natural world has given rise to a political ecologism, known as Green politics. Among its main concerns are: climate change and global warming, pollution, acid rain, the impact of nuclear and fossil fuel energy, and loss of species. Green politics is a political ideology that seeks to create an ecologically sustainable society and is rooted in environmentalism, non-violence, social justice and grassroots democracy. It emerged as a visible movement during the 1970s, and in 1979 the German Green Party (die Grünen) launched. Greens are generally to the left of the political spectrum. The movement shares links with other social and political movements such as feminism and the peace movement. Similarly, many political movements have developed environmental strands, for instance ecofeminism and eco-anarchism, and in the face of increasing environmental concern, so have most major political parties.

The Green movement

Inspired by books such as Rachel Carson's *Silent Spring*, the Green or environmental movement originated in grassroots activism. From this emerged a number of non-governmental organizations (NGOs), which have campaigned around various environmental issues, raising awareness and influencing organizations and policy. They include Friends of the Earth, which was launched in 1969 and today has 2 million activists in 73 countries, and Greenpeace, which emerged in 1971 and is known for its sometimes controversial dramatic direct actions. Because environmental issues are huge and often global, activists in the early days of the Green movement adopted the slogan 'think globally, act locally'. As a result, local grassroots activism continues to play a significant role in Green politics, focusing on issues such as fracking, GM crops and road building. While Green activism is now worldwide, Green political parties have struggled to enter mainstream politics. Even so, in 2009 there were 46 Green MEPs in the European parliament, and the UK elected its first Green MP in 2010.

Pollution, climate change and global warming

One of the Green movement's great successes has been to put environmental concerns onto national and international political agendas. However, raising issues and achieving change are two different matters, partly because tackling global warming, climate change and pollution is seen as having potentially damaging effects on energy and food production.

Since the 1980s, environmentalists have argued that human activities are changing Earth's climate, warning that emissions from fossil fuels coupled with deforestation are causing pollution, land degradation, damaging the ozone layer and raising global temperatures. In 1992, more than 100 heads of state and governments met at the Rio de Janeiro Earth Summit, reflecting the integration of environmental concerns into world politics. However, despite 1997's Kyoto Protocol, governments and global corporations have not met targets for reductions in greenhouse gas emissions or developed internationally agreed strategies for tackling the problem.

Sustainability and resources

Moving towards sustainable development – the rational use of resources to meet current and future human needs, without inflicting irreversible damage to the environment – is a fundamental principle of Green politics. Since the Industrial Revolution, humans have relied on fossil fuels such as coal, oil and natural gas to power the increasing needs of industry and domestic use. However, these resources are not only finite but also major pollutants contributing to climate change and global warming.

Green proposals for sustainable development include strict conservation of resources and the use of renewable energy, such as solar, wind and tidal power, rather than nuclear power or continued extraction of fossil fuels. Opposed to GM crops, environmentalists campaign for environmentally friendly farming practices, conservation and a more equitable distribution of resources, pointing out that Western nations consume a disproportionate amount of the world's resources.

Ecology vs development

With their emphasis on ecology, environmentalists are often accused of denying developing nations access to the same wealth and sophistication enjoyed by industrial nations. Many argue that developing nations should be free to pursue the same economic paths as others have taken previously. Environmentalists, however, argue that environment and development are inextricably linked and cannot be treated separately. In the words of the 1987 Brundtland Report (*Our Common Future*), 'Failures to manage the environment and to sustain development threaten to overwhelm all countries ... Development cannot subsist upon a deteriorating environmental base.' All growth must therefore take into account the costs of environmental destruction. To this extent, environmentalists have promoted small-scale agricultural projects, the development of Fairtrade and an end to the Western world's dumping of dirty industries onto the developing world, which has resulted in a number of eco-disasters, such as occurred in Bhopal in 1984.

Other eco-movements

L ike other political movements, the Green movement contains people who have combined environmentalism with other beliefs. They include eco-socialists, Green anarchists and ecofeminists. Eco-socialism, also known as Green socialism, combines aspects of socialism or Marxism with environmentalism. Adherents argue that the global capitalist system causes not only poverty and social exclusion, but also degrades the environment and is wasteful of resources.

Green or eco-anarchism emphasizes ecology, as well as critiquing hierarchical and state structures. Influenced by the writings of American environmentalist Henry Thoreau and French anarchist Élisée Reclus, eco-anarchists argue that social reorganization must work with nature. Ecofeminism emerged in the 1970s; the term was probably first used by Françoise d'Eaubonne, who started a 'Ecologie-Feminisme' movement in France in 1972, declaring that the destruction of the planet was inevitable if power remained in male hands.

Deep ecology

Norwegian philosopher, Arne Naess, was the first to use the term 'deep ecology' in 1973, although environmentalists and conservationists were already thinking along these lines. It implies the need to examine ecology at a very deep level and determine the long-term consequences of human impact on the world. Politically, deep ecology also links with and informs other movements, such as animal rights and Earth First. Deep ecology is effectively the ecological and environmental philosophy underpinning Green politics. It places value on all living beings, irrespective of their worth to humans, and advocates a radical restructuring of contemporary human societies. For adherents, Earth is not human-centric but rather consists of complex interrelationships or ecosystems, within which each organism relies on the others – a view with echoes of James Lovelock's Gaia hypothesis, which postulated that the Earth is a living organism. Human interference with any part of an ecosystem, such as deforestation, damages the natural balance, posing a threat to all living things.

International politics

Governments are responsible not only for the internal, domestic affairs of the state, but also for its interactions with other states. The history of these interactions has been one of conflict – expansionism and defence – but also of alliances and trade. And the modern world of international relations is similarly divided into questions of conflicting national interests and international cooperation.

Traditionally, international politics was concerned with military might and territorial matters, but with the growth of trade has increasingly involved economic cooperation between nations for their mutual benefit. Today, globalization is a buzzword describing the apparent disappearing of national borders in international transactions, and the rise of transnational corporations with huge economic power. But while the world seems to become smaller, there are still political, cultural and economic divisions. Far from becoming homogeneous, the world population remains divided between rich and poor countries.

Diplomacy

International relations can take place at the highest level, between heads of state reaching agreements to avoid conflict, or working together on a matter of common concern, but normally the groundwork has already been done by their diplomatic services, who also manage relations between countries on a day-to-day basis. A section of the government department for foreign affairs in most countries is staffed by diplomats, who represent the state in its dealings with other nations. Some are stationed in embassies – branch offices of the government, in various other countries – from which they can communicate with the officials of that country.

The role of diplomats is to protect their country's interests, and the interests of its citizens, abroad. This sometimes involves resolving conflicts of interest to avoid war, but for much of the time is concerned with trade agreements and maintaining friendly relations between countries through social and cultural exchanges.

Foreign policy

The relationship a nation has with other countries is determined by the foreign policy of its government – the ways it interacts with them militarily, politically, economically and socially. Of primary concern is promoting and protecting the interests of the state, while ensuring peaceful relations with other nations. Foreign policy decided by sovereign states is supposedly free from outside interference, but in practice is shaped by the actions and attitudes of other nations. There may even be pressure from strategic allies or the international community to adopt a particular stance. Countries with superior military or economic power can influence smaller, less powerful nations, especially if they are dependent on foreign aid. Membership of defence alliances, such as NATO and the Warsaw Pact, aligned the political and military foreign policy of members with the superpowers of the USA and Russia. Transnational corporations can also affect the economic slant of a country's foreign policy, which is often developed in conjunction with partners in a trading bloc, such as the EU.

Defence and national security

The nature of defence and national security has changed dramatically with the advent of modern weaponry. Now war can be waged over long distances to devastating effect, the importance of international politics and diplomacy has increased. The Cold War that characterized much of the 20th century was based on the possession of nuclear and other weapons of mass destruction, and the notion of 'MAD' (mutually assured destruction). Deterrence, often in the form of a sabre-rattling arms race, prevented the kind of large-scale conflict seen in two world wars, but resulted in a large number of small 'proxy wars' using conventional weaponry. International agreements limit the use and proliferation of weapons of mass destruction, but old habits die hard and the old powers are reluctant to totally relinquish their weaponry. New threats come from terrorism, and many countries have responded by an increased emphasis on intelligence and surveillance to ensure national security, often seeking international cooperation in dealing with a global concern.

Expansionism

Some nations have been aggressively expansionist, seeking to expand their territory by invading and occupying other countries. Empires have been built by nations extending their boundaries, annexing neighbouring countries or colonizing distant ones. In the lead-up to the Second World War, the nationalist movements of Nazi Germany and fascist Italy were seeking respectively *Lebensraum* and *spazio vitale* – 'room for living' – and later the Soviet Union sought to extend its communist empire. Sometimes expansionism is justified as regaining a territory previously lost or that traditionally belonged to a particular people, but generally it is regarded as an unwarranted act of hostility, met with international condemnation and armed resistance. Nowadays, nations expand their sphere of influence economically rather than by force, gaining access to resources in other countries through trade. When this occurs between nations with unequal economic and political power, it can be seen as a legitimized form of subjugation and exploitation, no better than colonialism.

Alliances and neutrality

Alliances are common during wartime and may dissolve with the end of hostilities, such as the cooperation between the UK, the USA and Soviet Russia during the Second World War. But in the second half of the 20th century, two major military alliances emerged: the North Atlantic Treaty Organization (NATO), comprising most nations of North America and Europe; and, in response, the Warsaw Pact (officially the Treaty of Friendship, Cooperation and Mutual Assistance) between the countries of the Soviet Union and its satellites.

More recently, with the breakup of the Communist bloc, new alliances are being formed, with economic and trade alliances also agreeing to some mutual military assistance and cooperation, and the Non-Aligned Movement of mainly southern-hemisphere countries not associated with or against any major power bloc. In addition, a handful of states, such as Switzerland, have steadfastly maintained a strict neutrality, refusing to align with any participants in international conflicts.

Just war theory

There has always been conflict between nations and, despite an almost universal condemnation of the use of force, international conflicts frequently result in war. But can war ever be justified? This was a question first addressed by medieval Islamic and Christian philosophers, who came to the conclusion there is such a thing as a 'just war', if it satisfies three main criteria: it must have proper authority (declared by a state or ruler); just cause (to recover something that has been taken); and right intention (the goal of restoring the peace).

The idea of *jus ad bello* – the right to go to war – later became a matter for international agreement rather than moral philosophy, and more detailed criteria for justifiable use of force were established. These included the ideas of proper authority, just cause and right intention, but also added principles of proportionality, probability of success and last resort. The rules of *jus in bello* regulating conduct in war were internationally agreed by a succession of Geneva Conventions.

Convention

pour l'amélioration du sort des Militaires blessés dans les armées en campagne.

La Confédération Suisse, Son Altesse Royale le Grand-Duc de Bade, Sa Majesté le Roi des Belges, Sa Majesté le Roi de Danemark, Sa Majesté la Reine d'Espagne, Sa Majesté l'Empereur des Français, Son Altesse Royale le Grand-Duc de Hesse, Sa Majesté le Roi d'Italie, Sa Majesté le Roi des Pays-Bas, Sa Majesté le Roi de Portugal, et des Algarves, Sa Majesté le Roi de Prusse, Sa Majesté le Roi de Wurtemberg, également animés du désir d'adoucir, autant qu'il dépend d'eux, les maux inséparables de la guerre, de supprimer les rigueurs inutiles et d'améliorer le sort des militaires blessés sur les champs de bataille, ont résolu de conclure une Convention à cet effet et ont nommé pour leurs Plénipotentiaires, savoir:

La Confédération Suisse:

le Sieur Guillaume Henri Dufour, Grand-Officier de l'Ordre Impérial de la Légion

Pacifism and anti-war movements

The protracted and large-scale devastation of the First World War proved a turning point in international attitudes to war. It was the prompt for greater international cooperation to prevent similar conflicts, exemplified by the formation of the League of Nations, which later became the model for the United Nations. But it also acted as a spur to grassroots movements opposed to the concept of war and pacifist organizations in countries around the world.

During the First World War, some British conscripts refused to fight on religious or political grounds, and established a right to conscientious objection, which is now internationally (but not universally) recognized. The peace movement gained significant support in the wake of the First World War, but waned during the Second World War, which was seen as a more 'just' conflict. With the arrival of nuclear weapons and the Cold War, however, pacifist organizations flourished once more, and their influence helped to change US policy during the Vietnam War.

Globalization

Although 'globalization' is a recently coined word, the idea is not a new one. For thousands of years, people have travelled to other countries and established links for exchanging goods and ideas, and commercial trade between nations has long been a source of economic prosperity. What has changed, however, is the speed and ease with which we can communicate, travel and move goods around the world. International trade has expanded massively in recent years, helping to increase prosperity in the developed world. Interdependence between rich and poor countries has sometimes been mutually beneficial, but often the least developed countries do not benefit as much as their richer trading partners. There are a number of reasons for this: richer countries tend to trade with one another in higher value goods and services (often in trading blocs such as the EU), and with poorer countries to provide raw materials and cheap labour; and the poorer countries are often in competition with one another providing similar resources.

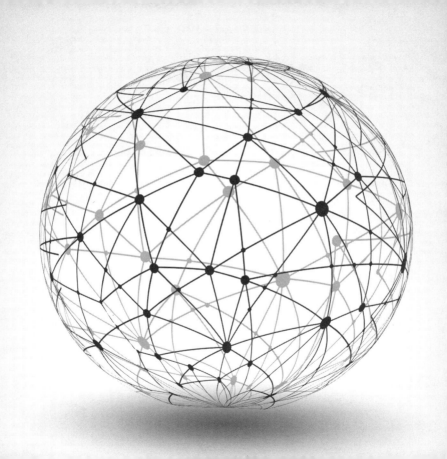

Transnational corporations

Transnational corporations (also known as multinational companies, or simply multinationals) sell their products around the world but tend to have their headquarters in one of the most developed countries, and factories or processing plants in less developed countries where production costs, especially labour, are much cheaper. This is, of course, advantageous to the multinational, but is also beneficial to developing countries, creating jobs, providing education and new skills, improving the infrastructure and generally assisting to develop the country's economy.

But there are disadvantages, too, not least of which is that the profits from these companies go back to their home countries, and only a little is reinvested. Working conditions are often very poor, since one of the attractions for the multinational is that there are fewer regulations on employment practices in poorer countries. Also, if the company decides to move out, the loss of jobs can cause major social problems.

Anti-globalization

Globalization offers the potential to reduce poverty in the less developed countries through international trade and the location of transnational corporations' production facilities. But unless regulated by international agreements the benefits are heavily one-sided. Unfair trade deals and exploitation by multinationals hinder rather than help developing countries. Growing awareness of this continuing inequality has resulted in the formation of a movement opposing the injustice of this aspect of globalization. Loosely known as the anti-globalization movement, it would more accurately be described as a movement against corporate or neoliberal globalization, as its criticism is directed against the unregulated power of transnational corporations to maximize their profits by exploiting the resources and workforce of poor countries. It is not opposed to international trade per se, and one offshoot of the movement has been the establishment of the Fairtrade Foundation to ensure producer countries receive fair payment for their goods and labour.

International law

Until comparatively recently, treaties between nations have been strictly between the signatories, with no international recognition of their validity. In an increasingly globalized world, however, with much greater international trade and cooperation, the need arose for internationally recognized agreements and some laws to regulate international relations.

Some supranational organizations, such as trading blocs or defence alliances, have laws agreed by all the member states, but there are also truly international laws to which the majority of the countries of the world are signatories. These cover issues that are generally beyond the scope of individual sovereign governments – such things as international commerce, copyrights and patents, human rights, territorial disputes and the conduct of war. Matters of international law are decided in the International Courts in The Hague, established after the Second World War.

International institutions

The United Nations was established in 1945 to replace the unsuccessful League of Nations, with the aims of maintaining international peace and security, promoting sustainable development, protecting human rights, upholding international law and delivering humanitarian aid. It consisted initially of 51 member states, but has grown to a membership of 193 – virtually every nation in the world. Although it has no real executive or legislative power, the UN has considerable influence as a medium for expressing the views of its members, each of whom is represented at the General Assembly.

The UN's various roles are divided between its five principal, active organs –the General Assembly, the Security Council, the Economic and Social Council, the Secretariat, the International Court of Justice. Other specialized agencies, such as the International Monetary Fund, the World Bank Group, and the World Health Organization, are autonomous organizations that coordinate with the UN Economic and Social Council.

World government

Since the Enlightenment, various movements have called for the establishment of a world government, a global political authority. For some, this meant the domination of a single ideology, such as communism or fascism, but for others it was a utopian dream of world peace as a single nation. In 1954, peace activist Garry Davis set up the World Service Authority to promote global citizenship and world government, which continues to issue World Passports, despite not being recognized by more than one or two nations. At present, the world consists of some 200 separate independent nations and there is no institution with global jurisdiction. The International Courts can decide only on issues of international law, and the UN has little real authority over its members. It seems that even with increased globalization, the notion of a supranational government – let alone a single world government – is still a distant prospect. It is possible, however, that environmental crises, such as resource depletion and climate change, may hasten further international cooperation.

The future

Human history can be told in terms of political change – often slow and gradual, but sometimes sudden and revolutionary. Recent rapid improvements in communications and transportation have facilitated globalization, and some form of liberal democracy is now the norm in almost every country in the world. While the spread of free-market ideology has undoubtedly brought increased prosperity, the gap between rich and poor has widened – both within countries, as well as between the developed and the developing worlds. This upward distribution of wealth, bolstered by government bailouts and harsh austerity measures, has contributed to a feeling of 'them and us'. As disillusionment with the prevailing ideology and conventional politics grows, politicians are perceived as being out of touch and acting in the interests of a rich and powerful minority. Popular movements, such as the Occupy movement with its slogan 'we are the 99%', have emerged with an anti-capitalist and anti-globalization agenda, and some economists have proposed alternatives to the neoliberal orthodoxy.

The future of the right

Since the 1970s, the neoliberal policies espoused by Ronald Reagan and Margaret Thatcher (see page 180) have been adopted by governments around the world. Strictly laissez-faire economic policies, combined with a right-wing social agenda, seemed to be a recipe for success, and at the turn of the century business was booming under these capitalism-friendly policies. In 2007, however, the cracks began to show, and the following year came a massive financial crash followed by years of global recession. The principle of minimal state interference in the markets had to be waived, as governments were called upon to bail out financial institutions that were 'too big to fail'. The majority of governments in the West believe free-market economic policies encourage growth and innovation, and rather than tax and regulate business to effect a recovery, imposed aggressive 'austerity' measures to cut public spending. The right, it seems, is moving further from the centre both economically and socially, and whether this has the desired effect remains to be seen.

The power elite

In 1956, the sociologist Charles Wright Mills published *The Power Elite*, which described the real governing power in the world as in the hands of a political, military and commercial elite. Despite the widespread adoption of some form of representative democracy, political power is largely handed over to these institutions who determine the political, military and economic decisions of the country. Increasingly, with unregulated free markets, large corporations have become dominant players, exerting influence on governments and even the military to act in the interests of commerce.

What Wright Mills did not foresee perhaps, was the emergence of a fourth institution as part of this elite, the media. With the traditional press, radio, TV and internet, media companies control the valuable commodity of information, and as these rapidly became part of a few massive multinational corporations, considerable political and economic power has been transferred to the media moguls.

The future of the left

At one point in the mid-20th century, something like one-third of the world's population lived in countries governed along Marxist principles, and elsewhere more or less socialist parties thrived in liberal democracies. But by the end of the century, the 'clash of ideologies' between the capitalist West and communist East seemed to have been won, with the collapse of the Soviet Union, the fall of the Berlin Wall and even the adoption in China of a modified form of capitalism. Communism was seen as a failed experiment, although some held that true communism had never been put into practice, and that the so-called communist states were in fact 'socialist dictatorships'. In the wake of this failure, many left-of-centre movements and parties abandoned socialist ideals, such as state ownership of industries and a government-led economy, in favour of free-market capitalism, even adopting some of its attitudes to welfare spending. However, as increasing inequality and austerity become more apparent than prosperity, there are signs of a resurgence of Marxist-inspired politics.

Power to the people

By the end of the 20th century, it seemed that the dream of government of, by and for the people was about to be universally realized. But the reality has proved rather different. In the 21st century, there is a widespread feeling that power still remains with an elite, the product of the free-market economics adopted by liberal democracies. In the global recession following the financial crisis of 2008, there was an increasing distrust of politicians (of all parties) who were seen as colluding with big business, and a disconnect between government and the wishes of the people.

Democracy, it seems, has not been achieved, and possibly always will remain an unattainable goal. The cynical view is that representative democracy is the best of a poor choice of political systems, and that the majority of people are happy to delegate responsibility for managing the state to an elected few. Besides, even in the most egalitarian societies, some form of leadership always emerges.

The political economist Francis Fukuyama dubbed what he saw as the culmination of social and economic evolution to an ideal political system, 'the end of history'.

A shrinking world

As well as the economic effects of globalization, profound changes have been brought about by improvements in communication and the ease with which people can move around the world. Populations in many countries have become more diverse as a result of immigration, while at the same time alliances of all sorts between countries have created a homogeneity blurring national borders. Yet people continue to feel a need to identify with a community. While some political groups resist change to traditional national identities, fearing conflict between indigenous and immigrant cultures, others welcome the development of pluralist societies. In the Western world, a balance is being struck between integration and multiculturalism that despite inevitable tensions, has led to people identifying themselves not in relation to a single cultural community, but several. There is no contradiction today in a person describing him or herself as European, British, Scottish, black and Muslim, any more than the so-called 'hyphenated Americans' – immigrants who have retained their cultural roots.

Religion in 21st-century politics

It is estimated that some 75 per cent of the world's population identify themselves as belonging to one religion or another. Even though only a few countries have an official state religion, the culture of many nations is shaped by the predominant religions, which undoubtedly influence their politics. In liberal democracies, particularly those with diverse multicultural populations, freedom to practise religion is considered a human right, but opinion is very much divided as to what role religion should play in affairs of state.

Even in avowedly secular states, such as the USA, a majority of voters find the idea of an atheist in the White House unacceptable. The intimate link between religion and culture is especially strong in more conservative politics, and this often means territorial, ethnic, or political conflicts have a religious dimension too; troubles in Ireland, the Balkan states and the Middle East are frequently cited as religious clashes when there are more complex causes.

Brave New World

It is likely that the accelerating advances in technology today will bring unforeseen changes not only to the way we live our lives, but also to the way we organize our societies. It has been suggested that we are moving into a post-industrial world based on information technology and, while it is true that much of the developed world has shifted to service industries, we are still reliant on manufacturing and agriculture. Information, and the speed and ease with which we can access it, is changing the way that we participate in the political process. Opinions are shaped by information spread through the internet, and this has enabled grassroots movements to thrive.

Mainstream politics has been slow to adapt, allowing many anti-establishment groups, including terrorist organizations, to infiltrate political and military computers. Some of this activity has exposed corruption and abuses of power, but also compromised national security, and has led to governments restricting civil liberties on the pretext of security.

In 2012, Julian Assange, co-founder of the controversial website WikiLeaks, sought refuge from extradition proceedings in London's Ecuadorian embassy.

The ultimate challenge?

Modern political theory and philosophy has concentrated largely on different attitudes to economic and social issues, and the degree to which these should be the responsibility of the state or the individual. The implicit assumption is that politics is a human invention, and as such can be determined by us. It has become increasingly apparent, however, that there are external, environmental factors that affect our political decision-making. Scientific evidence points overwhelmingly to the fact that our previous management of the environment has pushed us to the brink of catastrophe.

Many mainstream politicians have made some concessions to Green policies (see page 352); others have chosen to ignore – or even flout – the warning signs. There are those who believe that drastic measures are needed to avert irreversible damage to the environment, which threatens economic mayhem and even extinction of our species. Unless these are prioritized now, they could very soon be the only item on the agenda.

Glossary

Anarchism
The belief that government is unnecessary, and even harmful, and advocates instead a society based on voluntary cooperation.

Authoritarianism
Any form of government based on the imposition of authority demanding blind obedience, as opposed to individual freedom

Bureaucracy
The system or institutions of government administration, staffed by (non-elected) officials

Capitalism
The economic system in which trade and industry are wholly or mainly privately owned and operated for profit

Coalition
A formal agreement to co-operate between political parties. A coalition government, in a parliamentary system, is one in which two or more political parties come together to form a government

Communism
A socio-economic political system in which all property is owned by the community, and individual citizens contribute according to their ability, and receive according to their needs

Conservatism
The political ideology that seeks to retain traditional institutions and values, in particular the hierarchy of authority and inheritance, and to resist political and social change

Constitutionalism
The belief that a government's power should be given and limited by a body of laws, the constitution, and its legitimacy is dependent on observation of these laws

Democracy
The form of government by the people or their representatives

Despotism
The form of government in which an individual or small elite rules with absolute power. The absolute ruler is often known as a dictator, or more pejoratively as a tyrant

Ecologism
The political ideology asserting that ecological and environmental issues should form the basis of political, social and economic systems

Executive (see
Separation of Powers)

Fascism
An authoritarian form of
government emphasising
the primacy of the state,
extreme nationalism,
strong leadership and
militarism, associated
specifically with Benito
Mussolini's National
Fascist Party in Italy

Federalism
"A system of government
in which power is divided
between a central
government and smaller
political units, such as
states or provinces

Feminism
The collective term for
the various movements
advocating and
promoting equal social,
economic and political
rights for women

Fundamentalism
The belief in strict
adherence to a doctrine,
in particular to traditional
religious dogma

Globalisation
The increased
interdependence of
nation states, and the
free movement of goods,
money and labour across
international borders

Government
1. The system by which a
state is ruled
2. The group holding
executive power in a state

Governance
The way a government
governs; more specifically,
the way in which policies
are established and
their implementation
monitored

Hegemony
The dominance of one
state, group or ideology
over another

Ideology
The system of beliefs
and ideas underlying
a particular political or
economic theory, and
forming the basis
for policy

Judiciary (see
Separation of Powers)

Just War Theory
The doctrine that aims
to ensure the moral
justification of war
and the way in which it
is fought

Left wing
The political ideologies
tending to advocate
policies of social equality,
social welfare and
government intervention,
such as socialism and
communism.

Legislature (see
Separation of Powers)

Liberal Democracy
A form of representative
democracy characterised
by protection of the
rights of the individual,
free and fair elections,
and a separation of
powers

Liberalism
A political ideology
based on the freedoms
and rights of the

individual citizen. In the US, the term "liberal" is now used loosely (and often pejoratively) as synonymous with "left wing"

Libertarianism
The political philosophy advocating liberty and the exercise of free will, with little or no government intervention; this can range from laissez-faire market capitalism to utopian socialism and anarchism

Marxism
The economic and political philosophy of Karl Marx, focussing on class struggle, and the transition from capitalism to communism

Meritocracy
Government by people selected according to merit, for their particular abilities

Monarchy
Literally, the system of government by a single ruler, usually referring to the rule of a king or queen

Nazism
The ideology of the National Socialist German Workers' Party led by Adolph Hitler, a form of fascism involving racist nationalism, imperialist ambition, and state control of the economy

Oligarchy
Government by a small group, or a dominant clique, family or class

Opposition
In a multi-party democracy, the major party or parties opposed to the governing party

Parliament
An assembly of elected representatives, usually the legislative authority of a state or multinational organisation

President
The elected head of a republic, the highest executive officer of a republican state

Realpolitik
Politics and diplomacy based on purely practical considerations, rather than philosophy or ideology

Republic
A state governed by elected leaders and an elected president, in which the people are citizens rather than subjects

Revolution
The overthrow and replacement of a government or political or social system, often by force

Right wing
The political ideologies tending to advocate conservative policies, with an emphasis on law and order, individual rights, free market economics, and non-interventionist government

Separation of Powers
Division of political power among separate, independent bodies: typically a legislature with the power to enact, amend, and repeal public policy; an executive with responsibility for the daily administration of the state; and a judiciary, with a system of courts to apply and interpret the law

Social Contract
The implicit agreement between the governed and the government to cooperate for mutual benefit and to give up some individual liberties in return for protection by the state

Socialism
The political ideology based on common ownership of the means of production and the abolition of privately-owned, profit-based trade and industry

Sovereignty
The right of a state to govern itself without outside interference; the authority a governing body has over such a state

Theocracy
Government by officials representing a religious authority, often clerics or priests, ruling by divine guidance and according to a specific religious doctrine

Totalitarianism
A form of government in which the political authority imposes absolute centralised power; citizens are subordinate to the state, and opposition is suppressed

Utopianism
Belief in the possibility of creating an ideal society, generally along socialist or anarchist lines

Index

Quercus

New York · London

ISBN 978-1-68144-479-6

Library of Congress Control Number:
2016933572

Distributed in the United States and
Canada by Hachette Book Group
1290 Avenue of the Americas
New York, NY 10104

Manufactured in Canada

10 9 8 7 6 5 4 3 2 1

www.quercus.com

Picture credits: 2: NASA; 9: Morphart Creation/Shutterstock; 11: Everett Collection/REX; 15: Florin Stana/Shutterstock; 21: Salvatore Barbera/Wikimedia; 23: © Matthew Aslett / Demotix/Demotix/Corbis; 27: Master Sgt. Cecilio Ricardo, U.S. Air Force/Wikimedia; 29: Tom Page/Wikimedia; 31: © Frans Lanting/Corbis; 33: Bibliothèque nationale de France/Wikimedia; 37: AndrewHorne/Wikimedia; 39: AJ Alfieri-Crispin/Flickr; 49: WPPilot/Wikimedia; 51: Graphic Compressor/Shutterstock; 53: Rob Wilson/Shutterstock; 55: © Hulton-Deutsch Collection/Corbis; 57: Maryna Pleshkun/Shutterstock; 59: Ivan Bandura/Wikimedia; 63: © Lucien Aigner/Corbis; 65: Elya/Wikimedia; 67: US Library of Congress/Wikimedia; 69: Yann/Wikimedia; 75: Jürgen Matern/Wikimedia; 81: Lisa S./Shutterstock; 83: AgnosticPreachersKid/Wikimedia; 87: Wikimedia; 89: U.S. National Archives and Records Administration/Wikimedia; 91: Everett Collection/Shutterstock; 93: Fabio Pozzebom/ABr./Wikimedia; 95: White House (Pete Souza)/Wikimedia; 97: David B. Gleason/Flickr; 99: Lalupa/Wikimedia; 103: Geographicus/Wikimedia; 105: Yann Forget/Wikimedia; 109: Redjar/Wikimedia; 111: © Brooks Kraft/Sygma/Corbis; 113: snig/Shutterstock; 115: zentilia/Shutterstock; 123: Arpingstone/Wikimedia; 125: Lawrence Jackson/Wikimedia; 127: © Pool/Reuters/Corbis; 131: Stocksnapper/Shutterstock; 133: © Adam Woolfitt/Corbis; 135: Runk/Wikimedia; 137: © Pool/Reuters/Corbis; 139: Hustvedt/Wikimedia; 141: Valua Vitaly/Shutterstock; 145: Tobias Koch/Wikimedia; 147: © Shepard Sherbell/Corbis SABA; 151: Liberal Democrats/Flickr; 153: Warren Goldswain/Shutterstock; 161: Eldad Carin/Shutterstock; 163: Matthew G/Flickr; 165: George Allen Penton/Shutterstock; 167: Urban~commonswiki/Wikimedia; 171: Shutterstock; 175: US Library of Congress/Wikimedia; 177: Allie_Caulfield/Wikimedia; 179: Ryan Lawler/Wikimedia; 181: NARA/Wikimedia; 183: Our Phellap/Wikimedia; 195: Scarletharlot69/Wikimedia; 201: Canadian War Museum/Wikimedia; 205: © Hulton-Deutsch/Hulton-Deutsch Collection/Corbis; 207: The Marcuse family/Wikimedia; 209: Manor 7812/Wikimedia; 217: Robert Crc/Wikimedia; 221: Philip Kanellopoulos/Wikimedia; 223: Nick Efford/Wikimedia; 225: © Julian Stratenschulte/epa/Corbis; 227: © Wally McNamee/Corbis; 229: US Navy Photo/Wikimedia; 235: Michael Würfel/Wikimedia; 249: US Library of Congress/Wikimedia; 261: Zhang Zhenshi/Wikimedia; 267: Keystone-France/GettyImages; 271: © Chris Trotman/PCN /PCN/Corbis; 273: Sean Locke/Photography/Shutterstock; 275: Roger Blackwell/Flickr; 277: © Randy Olson/National Geographic Creative/Corbis; 279: Mageslayer99/Wikimedia; 281: Daily Herald Archive/GettyImages; 287: National Archives (UK)/Wikimedia; 289: MEDIA24/Gallo Images; 291: US Library of Congress/Wikimedia; 293: Olivia Little/Wikimedia; 295: John Roman Images/Shutterstock; 297: Joachim Wendler/Shutterstock; 299: US Navy Photo/Wikimedia; 301: Israel_photo_gallery/Flickr; 303: Iahsan/Wikimedia; 309: WPA Pool/GettyImages; 311: White House (Pete Souza)/Wikimedia; 315: Juhu/Wikimedia; 317: myshi/Wikimedia; 319: Utente:TheCadExpert/Wikimedia; 321: Gage Skidmore/Wikimedia; 325: Menendj/Wikimedia; 341: SRA Gerald B. Johnson, United States Department of Defense/Wikimedia; 343: Anton Bielousov/Wikimedia; 345: Albin Olsson/Wikimedia; 347: Mm.Toronto/Wikimedia; 349: Alena Brozova/Shutterstock; 351: Prolineserver/Wikimedia; 353: Wknight94/Wikimedia; 355: ColorCS/Wikimedia; 357: Eye Steel Film/Flickr; 359: JJ Harrison/Wikimedia; 363: Sadik Gulec/Shutterstock; 365: Mic/Wikimedia; 367: Oleksiy Mark/Shutterstock; 369: US Department of Defense/Wikimedia; 371: NARA; 373: volkovslava/Shutterstock; 375: Swiss Federal Archives, CH-BAR#K1#1000/1414#2*/Wikimedia; 377: Flyingbird/Wikimedia; 379: Jozsef Bagota/Shutterstock; 381: Vincent van Zeijst/Wikimedia; 383: Sam Fentress/Wikimedia; 385: Lybil BER/Wikimedia; 387: United Nations Mission Geneva/Flickr; 389: Patrick Gruban/Wikimedia; 391: socialistalternative/Flickr; 393: © Andrew Winning/Reuters/Corbis; 395: David Shankbone/Flickr; 397: Michalis Famelis/Wikimedia; 399: © Colin McPherson/Corbis; 401: Baigal Byamba/Flickr; 403: Nancy Pelosi/Flickr; 405: Cancillería del Ecuador/Flickr; 407: Smudge 9000/Flickr.